IRONIC SAMUEL BECKETT

Samuel Beckett's Life and Drama: *Waiting for Godot, Endgame,* and *Happy Days*

Pol Popovic Karic

University Press of America,® Inc.
Lanham · Boulder · New York · Toronto · Oxford

Copyright © 2007 by
University Press of America,® Inc.
4501 Forbes Boulevard
Suite 200
Lanham, Maryland 20706
UPA Acquisitions Department (301) 459-3366

PO Box 317
Oxford
OX2 9RU, UK

Library of Congress Control Number: 2006929006
ISBN-13: 978-0-7618-3529-5 (paperback : alk. paper)
ISBN-10: 0-7618-3529-6 (paperback : alk. paper)

⊖™ The paper used in this publication meets the minimum
requirements of American National Standard for Information
Sciences—Permanence of Paper for Printed Library Materials,
ANSI Z39.48—1984

To my Hildas

Contents

Acknowledgments

I offer my most sincere thanks to Dr. Alberto Bustani Adem, Rector of the Campus and the Zona Metropolitana de Monterrey del Tecnológico, for his support.

Dr. José Ramón Alcántara Mejía encouraged me to persist in this project and made valuable suggestions.

My friend Dr. Wolf Kozel offered creative interpretations and hypothetical reconstructions of numerous dramatic scenes.

Dr. Richard Danner, Professor Emeritus of Modern Languages, kindly proofread the final version of this book.

The publication of this book has been made possible by:

Cátedras de investigación
Literatura Latinoamericana Contemporánea
Tecnológico de Monterrey, Campus Monterrey

Introduction

Although irony is not one of the predominant themes in the abundant critique of Samuel Beckett's drama, I would like to show how different concepts of irony mold Beckett's life and dramatic trilogy: *Waiting for Godot, Endgame* and *Happy Days*.[1] Irony gives a sense of cohesion and reflects the mutual influence between his life and drama. We shall see in Wayne Booth's critical analysis how the biographical information about an author could be used as an interpretive tool despite its controversial acceptance among modern critics. The biographical information that is presented in the first chapter will not be used in the analysis of the plays that this book proposes in the third, fourth and fifth chapters but it will be taken up again in the conclusion.

Irony, far from being a pejorative approach to criticism or life, is a liberating mechanism in the psychological and artistic sense as Plato and Kierkegaard suggest in their works. Plato uses the term *eiron* to refer to the ingenious Socrates who feigned ignorance during philosophical discussions, while Kierkegaard reveals the methods of ironic

---

[1] Samuel Beckett. *Waiting for Godot* (New York: Grove Press, 1972)
Samuel Beckett. *Endgame* (New York: Grove Press, 1958)
Samuel Beckett. *Happy Days* (New York: Grove Press, 1961)

reconstruction of reality that allow its author to free himself from the austere conditions in which he lives.[2]

In the second chapter, irony is presented as a mechanism that promotes relations between different semantic and semiotic levels offering a number of polyvalent messages to an individual or group. The individual or the group has the freedom to contemplate, interpret or ignore the information that contains an ironic message. Nevertheless, the ironic message contains a concealed threat for its author, not the narrator, as Socrates experienced in his own flesh.

Groups or societies which collectively classify irony as a deformation of the communicative means usually feel threatened by its implicit messages that are introduced into their social setting. The latent dread of the hidden message and the desire to suppress it impose the rule of "no right to say it". In the name of seriousness and explicitness, the group in power often tries to cancel the threat that irony represents.

Seen from the opposite point of view, irony provides a way of communication, catharsis and freedom that a person needs in order to survive in a world of permanent chaos and oppression. After all, the human being needs to preserve communicative and hence social ties with his or her *milieu*. This communicative bond is facilitated by irony despite some restrictive social norms.

The ironic message requires a receptor's decryption. This phase introduces the receptor into the codifier's world in which he needs to identify the signs. If the receptor does not manage to decrypt the system of signs, the message will remain beyond his grasp. If the codifier and the receptor manage to share the same "language", they establish a

---

[2] Both of these concepts will be seen in the second chapter and applied to the analysis of Beckett's drama.

special bond of communication. Beckett's drama invites the spectator to engage in this type of decodification.

In Beckett's dramatic trilogy, the protagonists express themselves directly just as their Irish playwright did in his personal life. Nonetheless, the irony of the playwright's life and work lurks behind the clarity of precarious situations and protagonists' explicit messages. A flagrant example of this contradiction can be seen in Beckett's academic formation and *goût* for literature that guided him toward a teaching vocation. We shall see how this lifestyle is incompatible with his state of mind as the depression, boils and drunkenness will ensue from his teaching career. The initial wish to teach at Trinity College and Professor Thomas B. Rudmose-Brown's unconditional support become Beckett's daytime nightmares. Dumbstruck by silence in the middle of his class, fleeing from the college the days of his expositions, hiding in his apartment and incapable to utter a word to the stupefied college administrators reveal the ironic reality in which a fulfilled wish was transformed into a punishment similar to the woeful fate of Hamm and Winnie.

The two opposite poles of Beckett's life are hidden and reproduced in *Waiting for Godot.* The protagonists, whose lives are based on awaiting Godot's arrival, flee and hide when they anticipate his entrance. The ironic overlapping of waiting for salvation that Godot brings and the fleeing that his possible entrance inspires is reflected in Beckett's waiting for the teaching position and his resignation. After years of preparation for the teaching career at the Trinity College, Beckett is terrified by and hides from his students as Vladimir and Estragon hide from Godot. Beckett's real-life situations and his dramatic scenes overlap allowing a free fluctuation from one side to the other.

In this trilogy, the dramatic aspects are based on existential issues from Beckett's life. The question of survival that the playwright has experienced before and during the Second World War is reflected in his work. The search for a possible solution in *Waiting for Godot* is based on the arrival, in *Endgame* on the exit, and in *Happy Days* on humanism. The existential search seems illusory in the first two plays, while in the third one, *Happy Days*, the hope sprouts from the sun-scorched land and overshadows the stage into which Winnie sinks. The Shakespearean motto, "to be or not to be", is incessantly reflected in the contradictions that overflow the parameters of Beckett's mind and invade his dramatic space.

We shall tentatively define the parameters of Beckett's irony and humanism during the analysis of survival in the trilogy. The protagonists' affective and psychological contradictions are entwined with the polyvalent dramatic signifiers and their cumulative product represents the ironic, human situation. The protagonists are immersed into the world whose complexity transcends their comprehension but they continue their search for solutions.

Samuel Beckett's Life and Work

Bibliographical Notes

It may seem pretentious to write about the life of a writer or playwright whom one has not met in real life but this study seems necessary and useful from critical and psychological points of view. Critics have written a myriad of texts on Samuel Beckett's life and work, which in large part coincide on the essential points.

Among the contributions that comply with a refined sense of psycho-philosophical comparison between Beckett's personality and his work, the mystically elaborated publication *Beckett, Entre le refus de l'art et le parcours mystique* stands out.[1] The oxymorons "silence-utterance" and "movement-stillness" find their ephemeral equilibrium in this complex literary contribution. Concluding the reading of this analysis, the reader establishes the ironic relation between Beckett's intention to conclude his work with silence and his sixty-year-long effort to write, publish and stage figments of his creation.

---

[1] Georges Godin and Michaël La Chance. *Beckett, Entre le refus de l'art et le parcours mystique* (Canada: Le Castor Astral, 1994)

Samuel Beckett by Alfred Simon is an equally impressive critical work on Beckett's life and work.[2] Simon reflects on the ever-changing critical perspectives on Beckett's drama. The new perspectives and comparisons confirm the playwright's perennial relevance to social changes. Among a number of ideas and interpretations, Simon elaborates the concept of "mort-vivants"[3] in Beckett's work in which he sees the unquestionable link with the holocaust. Simon's polyvalent reflection promotes the analysis of Beckett's work from mainly sociocultural, structuralist and political points of view. The diversity of perspectives in Simon's work manifests Beckett's potential to inspire the gestation of new interpretations and associations.

The World of Samuel Beckett by Lois Gordon adopts a historical and geographic perspective which entwines with Beckett's biographical path.[4] Gordon analyzes Beckett's personal and professional formation through his links with the socio-cultural settings of the countries in which he lived. According to Gordon, the Irish socio-political setting in the beginning of the 20th century, the 1916 Irish Rebellion, nationalisms, militias, as well as horrors and heroism in continental Europe during the Second World War provide the raw material for Beckett's ideological formation.

Samuel Beckett by Deirdre Bair has a much more personal focus on the author than the previously cited works.[5] The meticulous precision and revelation of the most intimate details about Samuel Beckett's life could offend a reader as the author often oversteps the bounds of propri-

---

[2] Alfred Simon. *Samuel Beckett* (Paris: Belfond, 1983)

[3] Simon 132.

[4] Lois Gordon. *The World of Samuel Beckett 1906-1946* (New Haven: Yale University Press, 1996)

[5] Deirdre Bair. *Samuel Beckett* (New York: Harcourt Brace Jovanovich, 1978)

ety. Deirdre Bair's exacting investigation follows all imaginable paths that lead to Samuel Beckett. His nudity remains starkly exposed to any reader who decides to crack open this voluminous biography in which every *malaise*, every insecurity and every boil is irreverently exposed. This meticulous explorer, whose work has sprawled over more than seven hundred pages and in which she does not forgive anything to anybody, just as Beckett did not, has probably conjured the most personal biography of Samuel Beckett that has ever been written. Her work stuns the reader with the most personal information about the origin and nature of Beckett's medical problems.[6] The voyeurism and the incisive narration of this biography give the impression to the reader that he/she knows personally Samuel Beckett. The archaic literary stereotype about the reader's identification with the protagonist was resuscitated by Bair's narration. After surviving prolonged depressions and reiterative disillusions, the reader feels profoundly relieved when Jérôme Lindon offers to Suzanne Deschevaux-Dumesnil to publish Beckett's work in *Les Editions de Minuit*.[7] Even though the hope to see Godot remains unrealistic for most modern spectators of this play, the hope for salvation of Samuel Beckett was embodied in Deirdre Bair's book.

The proliferating studies of Samuel Beckett and his drama have a tendency to blend together like vines, and some investigations resulted in a repetition of already published concepts. Nonetheless, the biographical studies that I cited provided me with an interesting overview of Beckett's life.

---

[6] Bair 202.
[7] Bair 407.

Birth and Childhood

The dates of birth of renowned persons, born in the 20th century, are usually unquestionably defined. It is one of the few points considered objective, as most other elements are subject to personal interpretations of critics, journalists and friends. In Samuel Beckett's case, even the date of birth is shrouded in nebulous interpretations and assertions. Samuel's parents, William and May Beckett, registered the birth of their son on the 14th of June of 1906. Due to the high death rate of newborns at that time, the Irish required that the birth of a child be recorded one month after his actual birth. Consequently, the 13th of May of 1906 was officially registered as Samuel Beckett's date of birth. Beckett asserts that this date is erroneous because his parents had doubts at first about his survival and later on forgot to register him as a new Irish denizen. According to Samuel Beckett's unwavering assertion, the correct date of his birth is Holy Friday, April 13, 1906.[8]

In various bibliographical sources, the description of Samuel Beckett's parents, particularly his mother's, contrasts with the most remote possibility of forgetfulness or lack of respect for the official obligations related to the registration of their son's birth. On the contrary, the description of May Beckett reveals the image of a meticulous administrator who assiduously complies with the norms of a respected Protestant family that is well established in the heart of Ireland, Dublin. The contradiction between Samuel Beckett's declaration and his birth certificate presages endless controversies related to his work which will divide theatergoers into partisans and adversaries of his drama.

Samuel Beckett also has a dramatic perspective on his arrival to this world. "Dramatic" in the sense that, on the one hand, he steps back in

---

[8] Bair 3.

time and observes his birth from a spectator's point of view; and on the other, he emphasizes the coincidence between his father's untimely exit and his arrival.

> I was born on Friday the thirteenth, and Good Friday, too. My father had been waiting all day for my arrival. At eight p.m. he went out for a walk, and when he returned, I had been born.[9]

This coincidence of events, or their lack of coincidence, represents the structure of *Waiting for Godot*. The patient waiting for Beckett's birth and Godot's arrival are both ironic. In Beckett's case, the awaited babe is born when the father steps out; and in *Waiting for Godot*, the protagonists persistently wait for Godot who never arrives. In both cases, the waiting and arriving do not coincide.

If Beckett's birth remains hypothetical as both the father and the birth-certificate clerk fail to immortalize unequivocally the moment of the playwright's arrival, at least the babe's appearance is described in a similar manner by virtually all the witnesses. It is thin, blond and blue eyed. Samuel Beckett inherits the name, without any administrative inconformity, from his stillborn brother who preceded him by only one year. The sharing of the name and the proximity of the brothers' birth and death leave a permanent mark on Beckett's psyche.

Independently from his birth, Samuel Beckett describes his childhood with vague illusions to happiness and sadness blending with a predilection for solitude and the need to create his personal niche to escape from daily turmoil. Solitude will also mark many days in Beckett's life to come.

---

[9] Bair 4.

During the first years of Beckett's schooling, the isolation coincides with the penchant for long reading sessions and meditation. The initial inclination to the solitary lifestyle is reflected in his major works. During the rare interviews granted to the journalists during his laureateship, Beckett often alludes to sadness and loneliness during his childhood. These tendencies are not necessarily undesirable elements that Beckett would have canceled if he had been able but rather personal characteristics that coexist with his feeling of privacy.

During his childhood, Samuel Beckett develops a close relationship with his older brother Frank. The brothers share some private moments during their explorations of the outside world. Even though Samuel is four years younger than Frank, he is the leader in the dangerous games and often manages to involve his older brother in problematic situations. Taking into account that their mother has a hefty hand and does not waver at turning it numb during spanking sessions, the boys' adventures represent a double danger: the exploration itself and the ever-pending punishment.

The spirit of a daring explorer palpitates in Beckett's veins and he bravely approaches quaint occurrences to unveil their secrets. Prodded by curiosity to observe a gasoline explosion, the young man takes some matches, hides behind the house, and drops a match into the gasoline container peering expectantly into the darkness to witness the very moment of explosion. The explosion scorches Beckett's hair and eyebrows, terrifies Mrs. May Beckett and triggers one of the most intensive spankings. The punishment is staged to surpass the gasoline explosion in intensity and quell Samuel's wish to witness other ignitions. The fact that the tin was not full does not abate his mother's fury and this incident marks the beginning of a great rivalry between the adventurous son and the peace guardian.

Samuel's daredevil games occasionally terrify even his brother Frank. Samuel's burgeoning love for the flora and fauna lures him into bird watching in their natural habitat, and it even inspires him to imitate birds in their activities. Surreally perched at the top of a lush tree, as if he were at the rehearsal of a new play, Samuel spreads his arms and lets himself plummet, hoping that the branches cushion his fall. Unfortunately, gravity cancels his plans and he slams against the ground. Stunned by the impact and his brother's motionless body, Frank dashes to his mother's side in search of help. I wonder whether Samuel's attraction for the strange, new games in his childhood is reflected in the search for a new style in writing and an innovative dramatic representation in his maturity. His games and dramatic creativity have a stunning effect on the audience and constitute complementary parts of his personal and professional life.

Although there are different classifications of Samuel Beckett's socio-economic status in his extensive biographical publications, the information on the family's *modus vivendi* and their property is relatively consistent. Abundant "tea parties" by the swimming pool and the tennis court, social cricket games, a complete team of maids and nurses, and the location of the house suggest that the family has no financial problems. Mrs. May Beckett ensures that the family possessions do not figure as purely esthetic amenities and complements them with proper social rites that were required at that time in urban Ireland.

Without any premonition about her son's latent literary bent, May makes sure that all her neighbors, guests, as well as close and distant family witness the rigorous devotion with which her family abides by bon ton principles and attends religious services.[10] The devout manifestation of thankfulness before dinner and the prayer before going to bed punctuate the timetable of family life.

The children's strict observance of propriety while receiving visits is quintessential for the family's proper projection into the Dublin society.

---

[10] Gordon 9.

The children meticulously observe the norms when welcoming, mingling and bidding good-bye to guests. The automatic reverences, courteous comments, pleasant smiles, the jovial tone and other respectful gestures are mandatory; and Mrs. May Beckett punishes severely the least deviation from the code.

Frank upholds meekly the family principles and Samuel is often punished for his inconformity with the rules. According to Bair, the incompatibility of Samuel Beckett's behavior with his mother's expectations starts at the playwright's age of three and ends at his mother's death. The friction between these diametrically opposed personalities causes great harm to both of them. Samuel's pain and grunts will be more extensively exposed in biographical literature as he will be crowned by the laureate. In the public eye, Samuel's feelings will overshadow those of his mother, just as the mother's hand covered Samuel's "bt'm"[11] with shadowy bruises during his rebellious youth.

The Beckett brothers receive a Spartan education. On the one hand, the religious and social principles inculcated by the mother; and on the other, the vigorous athletic training imposed by the father. He hurls them into the water without any previous training, presupposing that his kids have an innate, ducklike ability to swim. After some erratic efforts to remain afloat, the children learn to swim. Later in their lives, they manifest the same vehemence in learning tennis and cricket.

The brothers often surpass their counterparts in athletic meets. In tennis tournaments, the Beckett contenders do not settle for a nicely placed ball which throws off their opponents. They push their game strategy one step further, converting the heads of their adversaries into

---

[11] Samuel's nanny finds the term "bottom" too vulgar and unacceptable for the Beckett household. And she gives it a much subtler nickname depriving it of the immoral sound "o". Hence the word "bottom" is transformed into "bt'm". Bair 19.

mobile targets. The hapless boys, confronted by the Beckett fury, often lose the spirit of competition and focus on their physical well-being. Samuel Beckett never revealed the inspiration for this athletic tactic but its origin might be traced back to his mother's training methodology, which was equally swift and efficient.

Formal Education

At the age of five, Samuel Beckett starts attending Ms. Ida Elsner's academy. Mrs. Beckett hand picked the school which was directed by the German spinster in order to ensure the proper continuation of her children's upbringing. Ms. Elsner amply fulfills the mother's expectations as the discipline takes the first place on the scale of importance, brushing aside educational goals.

Later, the brothers attend the Earlsfort House School whose director is a proud Frenchman, Monsieur Le Peton. This choice is not surprising as the Irish high class and those who aspired to be a part of it had a bent for the French culture and accorded preferential consideration to its teachers and nannies.

Monsieur Le Peton offered the coveted bilingual education and combined it with the Spartan spirit that he upheld with a dreadful paddle. Samuel refers to this object of disciplinary reinforcement with a vague connotation to sadism as the French educator, according to the playwright, seeks excuses to unleash the paddling frenzy. The image of Monsieur Le Peton slapping the palm of his hand with a white glove is engraved on Samuel's memory as a symbol of this institution in which the excuses for triggering the Frenchman's fury are as abundant as the glove stokes.

At the age of thirteen, Samuel follows his brother Frank to Portora Royal School in Enniskillen, Northern Ireland. Frank's conformity with the rules and Samuel's rebelliousness manifest themselves anew. Samuel prefers solitude in which he seeks refuge from the daily turbulence. The stepping outside of the social commotion allows him to grasp with greater plenitude the social profile of his community, which will be expressed in his drama and prose. Nonetheless, when he decides to participate in the social events, he becomes his classmates' leader.[12] The intense participation in social events and the shying away from them represent the two sides of the same coin; in other words, Samuel Beckett's personality.

Samuel's relationship with teachers is far from being exemplary as his scorn for authority is overwhelming. The safety valve that responds to his increased tension spews the accumulated pressure in the form of mockery. In 1920, the article "Some Home Truths About the Ancients", albeit signed "Bat", points in Samuel Beckett's direction. In this publication, adopting a sophisticated style in the description of the Emperor Julius Caesar, the author mocks Professor Thomas Murfet, who teaches classical literature. This teacher, like many others to follow, becomes a target for Samuel Beckett's caricatures and hoaxes. He hones his tennis strategies and indulges in indiscretion and gives free rein to his rebellious impulses. As was his wont, Samuel Beckett approaches his target directly and unleashes his full wrath without any consideration for his victim.

The mathematics teacher Mr. Tetley is also a constant nightmare in Beckett's life; the subject matter and his representative threaten Beckett's predilection for chaos and disorder. Manifesting his need to quell the inner turmoils, Samuel decides to caricature his *bête noire*. One after the other, the caricatures take shape in his notebook. Beckett invites the teacher to take a

---

[12] Bair 27.

peek at them and at the same time hides them from him. When finally Mr. Tetley's patience is worn out, he approaches the student who pretends to cover his notebook. Samuel Beckett's work of art stuns the teacher, leaving him dumbstruck in the middle of the class with a gaping expression on his face. Inspired by a wicked impulse, Samuel had drawn a caricature of Mr. Tetley with his legs spread out and bending over to the point of looking backward between his legs. The emphasis of the brazen artist is placed on the prominent buttocks of the teacher. Seen from a psychoanalytical point of view, this caricature could be a reaction to the Puritanism of the nanny whose sense of propriety imposed the abbreviation of the word "bottom" to "bt'm". Hence Samuel's reaction is to enlarge the buttocks beyond real proportions. The indiscretion hurt Mr. Tetley severely, and even Samuel's classmates felt sorry for the teacher. This incident is not an accidental excess of creativity but Samuel's reaction to the rigid and yokelike social structures of his environment.

Beckett's academic results at Portora are not laudable but he manages to comply with its minimal requirements. On the other hand, he leaves an indelible mark on the athletic charts. He wins easily the boxing tournament in the light heavy-weight division and leads his teammates to victory as the captain of the cricket, swimming and rugby teams. Besides athletic feats, the privilege to play piano sets him apart from the rest of the students. Half a century later, his classmates from Portora will remember the tall and elegant student who used to play piano.

Ironically, Samuel Beckett does not shine in writing or other academic fields but he impresses coaches and audiences in sports and music. Samuel's athletic and musical rhythms will conjure in his plays a special aura. Winnie will listen to music while sinking into the stage and steps will often echo on the stage of different representations punctuating time. Experimenting with different methods of representation, Beckett will warp the melody of Schopenhauer's music and disrupt the rhythm of his swimming stroke. At times, these changes take the form of silence and immobility to permit the spectator to fill in the dramatic space with his own rhythms and thoughts.

Youth

At the age of seventeen, Samuel Beckett starts taking classes at Trinity College. His approach to public relations has become somewhat more conservative but his mediocre academic results persist. His tutor, Dr. Arthur Aston Luce, remembers the mediocrity of this taciturn student and the need to motivate him. Samuel Beckett's academic impression leaves so much to wish for that he has to take some extracurricular exams, which were designed for the students with serious deficiencies.

Professor Wilbraham Trench's eloquent presentations on the imposing work of William Shakespeare leave the young man indifferent. During these lectures, Samuel idly counts the number of times Professor Trench repeats mechanically "at all".[13] Samuel's new pastime at least cancels his drawing impulses.

The social contact between Samuel Beckett and his professors and other students does not suffer any unusual setbacks. His aloofness takes the guise of the Trojan horse that does not serve to break into a closed society but to remain in its outskirts. During the third year of Beckett's studies, he increases the distance between himself and his family, becomes even thinner, and his mother is forced to coordinate weekly shuttles to her son's confined premises to bring him his favorite foods. Pressured by the untimely visits of his mother, Samuel accepts the provisions courteously and bids her farewell before she sits down. She strug-

---

[13] Bair 38.

gles to bridle her anger in order to partially offset Samuel's emaciation and to preserve the already tenuous contact with him. The mother's attention and her son's curtness create the setting for the arm-wrestling competition that was initiated in Samuel's childhood and extends well into his adult life.

During the third year of Beckett's studies, a critical transformation takes place in his formation. The study of languages and literature starts to compete with Beckett's cricket activities. The influence of the French professor Thomas B. Rudmose-Brown has a definite influence on the young man, particularly on his exegeses of *Divina Comedia*.[14] If we analyze Samuel Beckett's key works, it will be difficult to ignore the obscure thematic and stylistic air that filters through the stage planks as it rises from Dante's *Infernos*. Even though the human being is a labyrinth of multiple influences, the coincidence between the somber tone of *Divina Comedia* and the Nobel Prize winner's writing remains significant.

Professor Rudmose-Brown also influences Samuel Beckett's social life. The meetings and study sessions in the professor's house allow him to meet a wide spectrum of artists and writers. The introduction into the artistic and literary circles in Dublin starts to define Beckett's career but his sense of privacy is not altered by the new *milieu*. At parties, his solitary figure, leaning against the wall, incites the curiosity of the guests. The exact purpose or pleasure that these meetings provide remains a secret but Beckett usually remains present till their very end. He usually remains silent and avoids the gazes of other guests for whom he remains a familiar stranger. His presence could be interpreted as the tentative staging of *Waiting for Godot* in which the identity of "Godot" as well as the reason for his arrival remain unknown.

---

[14] The tone of this classic will have a strong impact on Beckett's formation. See how Dante and Vico influence Beckett in Godin 23.

During this period, the young man develops a taste for the stout Beamish[15] that, together with other alcoholic beverages, will accompany the playwright during his artistic *parcours*. It is possible that the lack of equilibrium in some of Beckett's protagonists, like Estragon[16], could be attributed to the effects that Beamish had on the author.

The sprouting of the penchant for literature is paralleled by the development of a bond with Professor Rudmose-Brown. The advice and support that the professor offers to Beckett reinforce his dedication to literature, drama and poetry.

The social activities change Samuel Beckett's academic performance and his image at Trinity College. He receives various prizes and honorary nominations in French and Italian classes that are crowned with the most coveted recognition: Foundation Scholarship[17]. His father was proud to see his son also honored on the cricket field during his third year at Trinity College. The recognitions in athletics and academia place Samuel Beckett in a spotlight.

Before starting the last year of his studies, young Beckett spends a summer in France. During long bicycle tours, the senior from Trinity College enjoys visiting Loire castles, museums and cafés. These experiences mark Samuel Beckett's life for good. His propensity for adventure, joke and exploration find an adequate setting in France. The French cultural elements and Beckett's experiences complement themselves in the young man's imagination and they will be reproduced in his writing.

After this trip, Samuel Beckett treads the Irish soil with a disdain for his mother culture. He peppers his speeches with French expressions and parades with his ostentatious beret. These changes in Beckett's appear-

---

[15] Beamish is a beer with a high alcoholic content.

[16] Estragon is a protagonist in *Waiting for Godot*.

[17] Besides the academic honor, this prize includes a considerable scholarship fund.

ance and behavior surprise his parents and friends, who occasionally smirk at the "frenchy".

At the end of the last year of his studies, Beckett starts a long friendship with a young Frenchman, Alfred Péron, who works as an English instructor at Trinity College. L'École Normale Supérieure and Trinity College had an exchange program which allowed a distinguished graduate of each institution to spend two years as a visiting instructor at the other university. Beckett and Péron quickly form a bohemian duo which seeks opportunities to experiment with life and literature.

Both intellectuals are accepted by the prestigious Modern Language Society (MLS), whose members constitute the intellectual cream of Dublin. The members of this society are proud of their social and intellectual status and expect sincere and profound thankfulness from Beckett and Péron for their admission to the association. In order to respond adequately to the society's expectations, Samuel Beckett convinces some friends to help him organize a grand presentation on Le Concentrisme, a new intellectual movement in Paris headed by Jean du Chas.[18] During this presentation, Beckett describes Le Concentrisme and its foundation in light of Rabelais' humor and humanism.

The days following this presentation, the society seemed to be revived by the momentum of the philosophical movement and Beckett's lively presentation. The members' comments on the drift and depth of Concentrisme lead to deductions about the civilization's harshness and its negative effect on humanity. Unfortunately, during the very apex of the intellectual gestation, a scandal erupts. The members of the Modern Language Society discover that "Le Concentrisme" is the product of Samuel Beckett's imagination and not the fruit of the contemporary French philosophers. This hoax was a slap in the face to

---

[18] Bair 50.

the members of the society and their erudition. Samuel Beckett's tendency to mock the authority and conventionalities reflects itself once more in this feat and foreshadows his future actions and drama stagings.

At the age of twenty-two, Samuel Beckett finds himself anew in the Parisian cafés sipping coffee and wine. The two-year period spent in the French capital as a Lecteur[19] of the École Normale Supérieure are strongly influenced by two men and two women. James Joyce represents the literary pillar and Thomas McGreevy a bohemian one. Peggy Sinclair is *la femme fatale* that inexorably attracts young Beckett, while Lucia Joyce pursues him. These four individuals represent respectively the cardinal points of Beckett's life: inspiration, entertainment, lasciviousness and a nightmare. Paris and these people form a unique entity which remains inseparable during Beckett's stay in the French capital.

These cardinal points make Samuel Beckett crisscross the city as if it were his backyard. It is a true miracle, comparable to Jeanne d'Arc's feats, that the young Beckett has enough time to write one line during the two-year stay in Paris. Furthermore, it is fortunate that the young man was able to survive these turbulent years as James Joyce's daily chores and Peggy Sinclair's wiles were sufficiently potent to push the most stable person over the edge of dementia.

In the French metropolis, Samuel Beckett follows Thomas McGreevy's steps. He is not only the Lecteur at the prestigious French university but also a distinguished bohemian in the city that is decorated with wine and liquor labels. The highly experienced Irishman in social activities introduces the tyro into the art of feasting, drinking and courting of Seine sirens. McGreevy's frequent invitations to a night in town abate Samuel Beckett's incipient depression and interrupt philosophical

---

[19] Foreign-language assistant.

elaborations about suicide. This theme is so intensely present in Samuel's mind that he takes advantage of every possible opportunity to provide new angles in its elaboration.

The members of the École Normale Supérieure are so fed up with Beckett's mournful presentations that they start to avoid him. As if Beckett's eloquence were not a sufficient threat to his social relations, his talent in flute playing, which used to reach its acme after midnight, almost inspired his colleagues to commit a collective suicide. It would have been interesting to combine Beckett's musical talent with the staging of *Waiting for Godot*, *Endgame* and *Happy Days*. The author's musical expression would have maybe shored up the existential foundation and the suicidal undertone in his plays.

Besides McGreevy's expertise in Paris night life, he is also a member of James Joyce's *coterie*. McGreevy introduces his young friend to James Joyce and these two literary minds automatically bond. Joyce discovers behind the elegant posture of Beckett a nimble and obedient mind that he quickly puts to practical use.[20] Samuel diligently complies with his new obligations. He becomes a punctual courier, a productive investigator and an obedient secretary. The young Irishman reads *Ulysses,* probably without understanding it, like most other readers, but he embraces it as a literary *chef-d'œuvre* of the twentieth century.

As James Joyce's eyes deteriorate, he retires from the outside world. He is endlessly bombarded by family problems but strives to realize his literary projects. When Samuel appears in his life, he gladly allows the young Irishman to write down messages, take notes, read texts, investigate, and describe the life in Dublin to him. Quite a few of Samuel's comments find their way straight into *Finnegans Wake.*[21]

---

[20] Beckett is twenty-four years younger than James Joyce.
[21] Bair 69.

Besides the practical help, Beckett also satisfies the psychological needs of his mentor. James Joyce is Catholic and during his childhood his family has belonged to the lower middle class. The financial constraint was a part of his family tradition and it remained an open wound despite his recent rise on the social ladder. The high-class scams and scandals intrigue Joyce but he never had an opportunity to witness them personally. What a fortuitous circumstance it must be to have a young Protestant, educated at Trinity College, volunteer his unconditional obedience to him. The young man who is used to pool parties and piano lessons bears down stoically during the most critical moments of his drudgery without uttering a complaint.

Samuel Beckett also starts imitating his idol. He enjoys mimicking Joyce's smoking gestures, he lets his wrist hang down as if he were dead and holds the cigarette with his fingertips. When reading, Beckett places his face close to the text as if he wanted to touch it with the tip of his nose, imitating Joyce's reading practice that was imposed by shortsightedness.

The mimic of James Joyce's gestures and practices is complemented by a masochistic trait. Samuel starts using the same size and shape of shoes as his idol even though they are too small for him. The blisters, calluses and swollen feet in the small pointed-toe shoes hobble Samuel's stride and deform his feet. In *Waiting for Godot*, Estragon will inherit Joyce's tight, pointed-toe shoes but he will abandon them faster than his creator.

Joyce's daughter, Lucia, is another source of martyrdom for the young Irishman. This young lady, inadvertently brushed aside by her parents, is in love with the equally confused Irish prince. The more Lucia strives to get closer to Samuel Beckett, the more he sidesteps her. Lucia's directness, nervousness and confusion are interesting for Samuel but only from a psychoanalytical point of view. The brash Irishman comments to his friends that the intensification of Lucia's nervousness and confusion will possibly culminate in a suicide.

During the daily conversations with Joyce, Samuel Beckett never expresses his disinterest in Lucia. He might have been waiting for Lucia to lose interest in him or simply fretted offending her father. He also might have considered that taking Lucia to the theater or movies was a part of his domestic chores.

The winding down of Beckett's stay in Paris intensifies Lucia's indiscreet coquetry. Nagged by the sharp pains in his feet or guilty consciousness, Samuel Beckett finally declares that the only reason for his presence in her house is to see her father. Beckett's curtness pushes Lucia over the edge of a nervous breakdown that turns into a deep depression.[22]

The furious mother immediately accuses Beckett of treacherously seducing her daughter. Her husband's posture remains rigid and solemn but his trembling voice and blood-shot eyes unveil a restrained fury. Joyce coldly informs Samuel Beckett that his presence is no longer welcome in his house. The "midpoint between irony and tragedy" is probably the best evaluation of Beckett's services in Joyce's home. On the one hand, Samuel intends to help the aging Irish author; and on the other, he opens Dante's gates of hell through which Lucia enters the domain of schizophrenia.[23]

On the opposite side of the feminine horizon, Peggy Sinclair places her bid on her cousin's affective spot. Her seductive wiles are fueled with Protestant and Jewish blood which wreak havoc among men. During the two-year stay in Paris, Samuel rushes to Kassel, Germany, every time he has an opportunity, forgetting the throbbing pain in his feet. In

---

[22] Gordon 77.
[23] Gordon 58.

good or bad health, full of hope or despair, Samuel shyly approaches his cousin's colorful skirts to clarify issues that he does not understand. Occasionally, accompanied by the melodies of her piano, the bohemian cousin allows Samuel to sit down by her side and share some sentimental duets with her. She even permits him at times to witness the courting of her German suitors. This culture of ostentatious sentimentality would have made Samuel's mother frown in disapproval but Peggy's mother considered it a normal aspect of her bohemian family. Peggy's games and magical voice that improvises and puns during her compositions derail Samuel's mind with greater ease than the French wines and Irish Beamish.

Lucia and May Beckett might have been able to learn from Peggy how to attract Samuel's attention but they did not. Samuel spends hours waiting patiently for Peggy to come back from her endless shopping chores, undertaken in company of her suitors, while he invents thousands of reasons for slipping out of his mother's and Lucia's grasp.

The time spent in Paris, 1929-30, is essential for Samuel's learning about himself and others. During these frivolous years in Gallic lands, the young man manages to publish his first works, an essay in *Our Examination* and the poem "Whoroscope". In these relatively short presentations, one notes a bombastic tendency but their production is a part of the learning process. The publications, even though pedantic for some readers, represent a great stimulus for the young writer. After the definite separation from the Joyce family in the summer of 1930, Beckett finds the time to sit down and write a longer critical essay on Proust which will be published during his stay in Ireland. Even though this study is more recommended to the critics of Samuel Beckett than to those of Proust, it represents the cornerstone in the young Irishman's literary formation that will lead to his great plays in the 60's.

Even though it might sound cynical, when Beckett leaves Paris, he knows which shoes to wear. This information will be very useful for him in the future as there will be many roads to tread on his way to the international recognition as a playwright and a novelist.

Professor and Vagabond

In the fall of 1930, Samuel Beckett returns to Trinity College. His return is far from being glorious as his analysis of Jouve was not written as meticulously as he had promised. Regardless of this failure, Professor Rudmose-Brown grants him the post of Instructor at Trinity College for the next three years. Despite this honorable position in Dublin, Samuel finds his reunification with his motherland deceiving. Ireland is passing through a period marked with strong nationalism and this cultural climate is adverse to Beckett's reincorporation into his home town. Once more, his tight suits and the beret that he bought in Paris contrast with the local attire and provoke curiosity and sarcasm.

Samuel is proud of his experiences on the continent and he does not hesitate to spice his speeches with gallicisms. The loftiness from which Samuel observes and comments about life, art, literature and politics of Ireland give him the air of pedantry. On one occasion, Samuel interrupts a discussion about a young Irish painter to pour out his venomous insolence: "A Veronicist who would wipe the face of Christ with a sanitary towel."[24]

The most serious obstacle that Samuel Beckett faces at "home" is his teaching profession. Samuel approaches this task applying the principles of silence and distance that he learned from James Joyce. He enters the

---

[24] Bair 116.

classroom, sits down turning his back to the students and faces the window. While waiting for the hubbub and the squeaking of the chairs to end, Beckett remains gazing steadfastly through the window as if he were spellbound by his cousin Peggy. Suddenly, he turns his face toward young ladies and before they recover from the start, he pronounces a highly cryptic statement which baffles them even more. A silence accompanies every statement, which allows the students to write down the exact citations of their teacher's *exposé*. The only flaw in their notes is the overwhelming incoherence.

Another of Beckett's *clins d'œil* is the unpredictable language switching. The constant flip-flop from English to French and vice versa completely disorients the students, who remain confused even when the professor speaks English. The linguistic shifts have been interpreted by some critics as a mockery of the young ladies' French but it could also be seen as the staging of a communication obstacle that is a part of Beckett's life, narrative and drama.

Beckett's jokes and mockeries are reproduced at Trinity College; but this time, he is their focal point. Beckett pretends not to heed some satirical publications in the university paper about a strange, gaunt, French-looking professor. He does not hear jokes and averts curious gazes while walking across the small university campus. These incidents, like Lucia's flirtations in Paris, send shivers down his spine. In order to soothe the painful effects of these impertinences and forget his students, Samuel Beckett consumes considerable quantities of dark beer. In the morning, he realizes that the miraculous beverage did not cancel his class despite the euphoric premonitions that he had felt the previous night. The numerous conflicts with students cause so many tensions that Beckett's mental state starts preoccupying his friends and family. His clothes become shabby and his cold seems implacable. The professor resembles a

Parisian vagabond in search of a drink that nobody seems willing to buy for him.

Until his definite separation from Trinity College in December of 1931, the flu and other physical symptoms of his psychological tensions defy all medical interventions. The ensuing depression is marked by painful boils on the back of his neck and in the genital area. They will serve for the rest of his life as a barometer of his internal pressure. Beckett's physical and psychological ills force him on several occasions to add a new dimension to the silent methods of teaching; he simply remains crouched in his bed, leaving his ungrateful students in an abandoned classroom. Under the cover of the night, he would stealthily sneak out of his apartment and disappear in one of the town pubs.

In November of 1931, Beckett's symptomatic sleepiness gradually increases. He remains in bed for several days, facing the wall in a fetal position. The administrators of Trinity College no longer try to cover up Beckett's pathological state because they need help from his friends and family to reanimate him. After several attempts, they manage to communicate to him that he can go to Kassel, Germany, as soon as he decides to get up. Samuel Beckett emerges from his lethargic state, gets out of bed and walks around the room while the visitors gape at him. Beckett's silence seems to be highly contagious.

On the eighth of December of the same year, Beckett receives his master's degree. A week later, on the last day of classes, he rushes to Kassel, Germany. As soon as he lands on German soil, he dispatches a telegraph to Trinity College announcing his resignation. He spends the following six months visiting the Sinclairs.

From 1931 to 1937, Beckett's life can be described with four words: frustration, alcohol, writing and hope. Two concepts influence his decisions during this period: the lack of money and the wish to escape from his mother. The want pulls him homeward and the sense of freedom in the opposite direction. In order for the mother to bring her dear son home, she diminishes and sometimes even cancels his monthly allowance. However, the slightest foreshadowing of Beckett's reincorporation into his family spurs his boils.

In 1932, Beckett realizes that if he wants to realize his dream of becoming a writer, he needs to earn his living and become independent. In the thirties, there is a proliferation of literary reviews in Paris and he starts publishing essays, critical analysis and book reviews. This line of work does not completely cover his financial needs that include unpredictable expenses in cafés and taverns, as well as trips to and from France, Germany, England and Ireland. During this period, his father sends him money openly and at times behind his wife's back.

In Paris, Beckett establishes contact anew with the Joyce family as Lucia is residing in a mental hospital and her parents need help in literary and domestic issues. This renewed contact starts again competing with Beckett's literary career.

Beckett's mocking impulse did not vanish; he writes *Dream* under the guise of a satire in which his acquaintances, friends and family play key roles. Beckett never dared publish *Dream* entirely but most of its chapters are included in literary reviews and *More Pricks*. Even the Sinclair family, that received him on several occasions and for prolonged periods of time, is subject to his brazen jokes. Beckett even includes *verbatim* Peggy's letter in *More Pricks*, in which his cousin writes English phonetically and with a heavy German accent.[25]

After publishing various essays in Paris, establishing contact with his buddies from the previous stays in the French capital, and being robbed in London, Samuel Beckett finds himself penniless again. In the midst of his anguish, he knocks again on his mother's door.

------

[25] Bair 165.

Little by little, his mother's silence and not so subtle allusions to a decent job enervate Beckett to the point of pushing him into a *maison de santé*[26] in which Lucia Joyce is hospitalized. Samuel dodges his mother's open and covert attacks by seeking refuge in Dublin taverns, and even sleeps in Clare Street when unable to walk back home. The disappointment caused by the scarce interest in his recent publications and the obligation to give private classes to young ladies in Dublin force Samuel Beckett to drown his sorrow in the Stout[27] that he carries in his pocket. Immersed in depression and loneliness, Samuel receives a letter from the Sinclairs informing him of Peggy's death. Tuberculosis stifled her in her sleep.

With his neck half paralyzed by boils, Beckett is getting ready to ask his father to finance his trip to continental Europe. But without any previous signs, his father suffers a heart attack. During five days, Samuel is completely absorbed by his father's illness. The attention focused on the father allays miraculously the son's ills. Helping his father, Beckett cures himself.

In June 26, 1933, after the doctor informs the family that William Beckett is doing much better, the patient dies. Only a few days after the father's death, boils cover Beckett's whole body. In pain and pus, the young man despairs and seeks refuge in alcohol. The sharp articulation pain and congestion do not respond to medicine and Beckett finds himself in bed. The nights become unbearable; his body wallows in sweat and his mind in nightmares. The erratic heart beat and suffocation wake Beckett, who finds himself in the state of uncontrollable panic and disorientation. After numerous insinuations and suggestions, Dr. Geoffrey

---

[26] Mental hospital.
[27] Stout is a heavy-brown brew.

Thomson finally informs the family that the young man's sickness is caused by anxiety and depression.

In January of 1934, May Beckett is forced again to allow her son to leave her home in order to be treated by the psychoanalyst Dr. Wilfred Ruprecht Bion. Beckett learns to analyze himself by reading Freud and Jung, and he discusses his findings with Dr. Bion. He realizes that his depression, academic elaborations of suicide and a variety of physical discomforts are only the symptoms of his psychological problems and particularly the feeling of being useless in a family of hard workers. During the sessions, Beckett seems to understand the need to be friendly with people, to keep a certain distance with his family and to play social games in order to earn his living as a writer and become independent.

On the 24th of May, 1934, *More Pricks Than Kicks* is published and receives relatively good comments in the press. This success fuels Samuel Beckett's optimism and helps him return home with an optimistic view of the future. He feels confident that the newly acquired skills in social relations will allow him to keep a certain distance from his family, friends and acquaintances. The new perspective, coupled with medication, helps him live in certain harmony with his family and friends. Samuel Beckett starts spending his afternoons in the National Gallery and talking to friends in Dublin taverns. Some of them are so stunned by his serene nature that they have to ask Dr. Thomson to explain it to them.

By the end of 1934, Beckett feels again profoundly lonely and dissatisfied with life but he manages to avoid major conflicts with his mother. As the year winds down, Samuel Beckett publishes several shorter works and decides to take a trip to London. In the British capital, Samuel receives several letters from his mother, who expresses a renewed pleasure in life and the need to close the period of rigorous mourning of her husband's death. After a thorough analysis of his personal and financial ties with his family, Beckett decides to return home despite Dr. Bion's advice.

Shortly after Beckett's return, May's optimism fades away. The tears and intense silence related to Samuel's aimless lifestyle alternate, and Beckett's boils flare up. The amiable and unintentional comments about a respectable job and an occasional mention of what her deceased husband Bill would like pepper the conversations between the mother and her son. The pragmatic lifestyle of Mrs. Beckett oblige, her to suggest to her son to seek the nomination for several posts in town, and she detains his allowance to help him make the right decision. During this period, Samuel Beckett takes a few breaks and travels to London and Germany. He also collaborates with several literary reviews and associations in Dublin.

In August of 1937, Samuel's brother Frank is getting ready to get married. The preparation for the wedding causes a lot of commotion in the house and May Beckett's mordant comparisons of the brothers infuriate Samuel. The skills related to the adequate social behavior suddenly get blotted out and Samuel seeks refuge in taverns.

In a moment of rage, his mother demands that Samuel abandon Ireland permanently. This declaration does not offend Samuel and he even tries to seal her decision or incite his mother to reiterate his excommunication. As soon as he gets out of bed where he was kept for ten days by a gastric flu, he recharges his batteries with the best Stout in town and smashes his mother's new car against an oncoming truck. As if the totaling of the car were not enough, Samuel Beckett initiates a judicial process that infuriates his mother.

The court clerks snicker and at times burst into laughter as they reread Samuel's official declaration of his innocence and the truck driver's guilt. The town rumors reach the climax on the day of the court's solemn ruling that of course does not favor the plaintiff. With the dramatic staging of the court saga, Samuel Beckett ensures his ticket to Paris. Some friends even comment about an extra allowance that is intended to make his trip more expedient and prolonged.

Even though the period from 1934 to 1937 is not marked by serenity in Beckett's life, he makes his most sophisticated literary contribution up to this point: *Murphy*. The novel's antihero is a typical Beckettian character. The principle of stasis and impassibility, which is reflected in Murphy, will be taken up again in *Waiting for Godot*, *Endgame* and in Beckett's life. There is an ironic relation between the principle of *stasis* and the tardy publication of the novel. After two years of searching for an editor and 42 rejections, Samuel Beckett's will withers like his protagonist Murphy.

On the 17th of January, 1938, the monotony of Beckett's life is interrupted by a strange incident. The local pimp, Prudent, approaches Samuel Beckett and insistently asks him for money in exchange for the services of one of his favorite stars. Annoyed by the pimp's touting, Beckett pushes the impertinent pimp away. The man falls down but promptly springs back and stabs Beckett in the chest. The knife pierces Beckett's chest and he drops to the sidewalk.

Beckett's mother and brother rush to visit Samuel. During numerous hours that the mother spends by her son's side, a new relation grows. Samuel promises among other things to spend at least one month at his mother's house every year. He will keep his promise and, surprisingly enough, there will be no major confrontations between the mother and her son after this incident.

The fact that Samuel Beckett feels at home in Paris makes him confident and allows him to receive his mother's visits and reciprocate them with relative serenity. Besides consistent sales of *Murphy*, Beckett starts to contribute regularly to literary reviews and newspapers that permit him to cover all his expenses.

One of the most riveting ironies in Samuel Beckett's life is related to his stabbing. By the middle of February 1938, Beckett confronts his assailant in court. Waiting for the clerk to beacon him into the courtroom, Beckett sits down next to Prudent in the hallway. After some moments of silence, Beckett asks Prudent why he stabbed him. The pimp responds in a manner familiar to most of Beckett's characters: "Je ne sais pas."[28]

The War

In 1939, Samuel Beckett enjoys for the first time a relative economic and affective stability. Suzanne is taking care of him and the sale of *Murphy* is satisfactory. The Irishman watches phlegmatically through the window the exodus of the Parisians who anticipate the Nazi invasion. In a moment of anguish, he feels the collective frenzy and starts trekking toward the south of France. A moment later, he stops, reflects and returns to his balcony. Beckett's contradictory impulses will be inherited by his characters.

The news about the torture and execution of several friends, particularly those of Jewish descent, stun Beckett and in October of 1940, he joins La Résistance Française.[29] During the following two years, Beckett works for the counterintelligence group Gloria despite the notorious pun-

---

[28]"I do not know."

Bair 283.

[29] Bair and Gordon have different views on the reason for which Samuel Beckett joins the Résistance. Gordon believes that Beckett starts to collaborate with the Résistance because of his humanitarian inclinations and Bair considers that Beckett is motivated by his friends' persecution. See Bair 308 and Gordon 140.

ishment for spying. His main activity consists of gathering information in occupied territory and dispatching it.

During the second half of 1942, the Gestapo infiltrates two principal *réseaux* (spying networks), Gloria and Prosper, and wreaks havoc among their members. Only twenty out of one hundred Résistance spies survived. After the war, hideous stories were told about tortures and blackmailing that befell the prisoners.

In 1942, Samuel Beckett receives a telegram that informs him that his closest collaborator was arrested by Gestapo.[30] This document disrupts Beckett's routine and he immediately abandons his apartment with his lifelong friend Suzanne. They spend several days in clandestine shelters and thanks to friends' help obtain sham papers, which allow them to undertake a long and tedious trip toward southern France. Hunger, cold and anxiety accompany the couple during a two-month odyssey to Roussillon, Vaucluse.

From November 1942 to April 1945, Suzanne and Beckett remain in a mountain shelter located in the free territory. During this period, Beckett goes through three major stages: anxiety, boredom and depression.[31] As there are no medical services, Beckett has to confront by himself his depression, schizophrenia, boils and insomnia.[32] His treatment is based on endless treks in the mountainous region of Vaucluse, the agricultural work in Aude and, more than anything else, the writing of *Watt*. In this novel, the protagonist's life constantly deteriorates, reflecting the author's situation. Reviewing his manuscript years later, Beckett hardly remembers some segments as if they were a product of somebody else's work.

---

[30] Linda Ben-Zvi. *Samuel Beckett.* (Boston: Twayne Publishers, 1986) 16.

[31] Watt reveals the same symptoms as his creator.

[32] Gordon disagrees with Bair's evaluation of Beckett's mental state. She particularly dissents with Bair's diagnosis of schizophrenia.

In Roussillon, Beckett initially refuses to participate in any Résistance activities which have brought him, as he says, to the point where he is. Under the pressure of the Maquis members, he ends up accepting to collaborate with the resistance fighters again. Among a variety of activities, Samuel Beckett accepts to hide a box of dynamite in the house that he shares with Suzanne, but he places it on the open balcony next to a geranium in plain sight of the people in the street. The intransigent decision to keep the explosives in the open scares Suzanne. She scurries around the house for a while and then runs out in search of their Résistance friends, whom she begs to come along and convince Samuel to change the "hiding place" of the dynamite box. Samuel generously complies with his friends' wishes but on another occasion chooses the same spot for the Maquis grenades and sends his friends anew into a state of frenzy. On this occasion, Beckett does not take into consideration any entreaties, and the anguish thumps in his friends' chests until the grenades are picked up by resistance fighters.

It is difficult to conclude what motivates Samuel Beckett to expose or hide the Résistance parcels on the balcony. Does he consider that the most conspicuous part of the house would abate suspicion or does he simply like to play with destiny like his friend Léon? Léon was Jewish and he decided to stay in Paris until his son's graduation. On the very day of the ceremony, he was picked up with the rest of his family. They were separated into different groups and deported to concentration camps. One way or another, Beckett sees life as a game in which he is the only one who knows the reason behind his acts, unless the acts are a product of his subconsciousness like *Watt*.

On the 30th of March, 1945, Samuel Beckett receives La Croix de Guerre for his collaboration with the Résistance. General de Gaulle personally signs this honorary document.

In April of 1945, Samuel Beckett finally leaves Roussillon. After visiting his convalescent mother in Ireland and setting up an extemporaneous Red Cross hospital in St. Lô, he returns to his Parisian apartment in the street Les Favorites, where Suzanne awaits him.

In 1946, Samuel Beckett seems to be cozy in the same apartment he occupied in Paris before the war. However, the interruption in his publications and a new exchange rate for the Irish monetary unit precipitate the couple into the old financial turmoil. From 1947 to 1948, the couple lives on the meager salary that Suzanne earns as a tailor but she never reproaches him their precarious financial situation. During this period, Beckett writes *Mercier et Camier*, *Molloy*, *Malone Meurt* and *Eleuthéria*.

By the end of 1949 and the beginning of 1950, Samuel Beckett tries to relax and get away from his depressing prose that racked his brains. Sipping wine, smoking, pretending not to care about editors' rejections of his manuscripts, Beckett writes a play, *Waiting for Godot*.[33] The tedious days and nights that Samuel Beckett and Suzanne spent in the streets, on the roads and in the countryside during their chaotic trip to Roussillon find their echo in this play. In numerous interviews and personal conversations, Beckett declares that this play is poorly written and that he undertook its writing only to overwhelm his boredom. Nevertheless, it will bring him undreamed glory and international prestige.

Dazzling Fame

In 1950, Samuel Beckett seems to be more disappointed than ever. His novels are rejected by numerous editors despite the optimistic comments of his friends and representatives. His literary representatives ended up

---

[33] Simon 42.

concluding that no publishing house will ever accept *Molloy*, *Malone meurt* and *L'Innommable*. Beckett hides from the world and himself during his daydreaming and nocturnal strolls. Suzanne realizes that without representatives Samuel will never be able to publish his manuscripts and decides to undertake the promotional task.

In the beginning of November of 1950, Suzanne is disheartened by the numerous rejections and starts manifesting the same depressive symptoms that plague Samuel. In a café full of smoke and with a cigarette in her hand, Suzanne awaits an employee of Les Éditions de Minuit to give her back three manuscripts. Instead of a courier, the director of the company, Jérôme Linden, appears and offers her a contract. Shaken by the offer, Suzanne does not understand Linden's patient explanations and re-explanations of the contract and asks for a few days to consider it. After a few days of recuperation from the shock, on the 15th of November, 1950, the contract is officially signed.[34] Even though the sale of the books is not exorbitant, the novels are sold almost without any interruptions since their publication.

Spurred by her managerial success and disappointed by Roger Blin's failure to gather the necessary funds for the staging of *Waiting for Godot*, Suzanne starts looking for a theater. She distributes the manuscript of the play to more than thirty theater directors, and the prevailing theme of waiting in *Waiting for Godot* becomes once more the metaphor of Suzanne's and Samuel's lifestyle. Unfortunately, no director expresses the least interest in staging such an outlandish and incoherent play. But after a series of fortunate *dénouements*, related to funds, theater availability and the selection of actors, the play rehearsals start in 1952.

The night of the play's première, Beckett seeks refuge in their countryside residence in Ussy. His nerves do not allow him to watch how his

---

[34] Bair 407.

life gets unveiled. Suzanne's attentive eye records the performance meticulously and reproduces it cinematographically for Samuel at their house. The première is an absolute success; the critics and the public coincide on the fact that they do not understand anything.

Since this performance, Samuel Beckett will never be abandoned by the swarms of reporters, journalists, American professors and playgoers who identify with Beckett's protagonists without understanding them or maybe themselves.[35]

During the following years, the fame expands exponentially and carries Beckett and Suzanne to the climax of international recognition. Samuel is enchanted and at the same time terrified by the scurrying that takes place in his apartment as if the journalists and critics wanted to stage a play of their own on the author's premises. As he probably could not hide in his bed the way he did at Trinity College because the reporters would probably keep on taking pictures of him in fetal position, Samuel often seeks refuge in their house in Ussy, leaving Suzanne to deal with the media.

The overwhelming mail, interview requests, friends visiting Paris and play performances in France, Germany, England and the United States drain Samuel's energy. He uses whatever free time he has to translate his work and write two major plays, *Endgame* (1956) and *Happy Days* (1960), as well as some books, essays and poetry. On the 23rd of October, 1969, the Swedish Academy offers the Nobel Prize for Literature to Samuel Beckett.

---

[35] It is important to note that the confusion never prevented academicians from writing on a subject.

In the early 70's, Samuel Beckett starts to lose vision like Pozzo[36], to become weak like Clov[37] and wanders away silently on the 22nd of December, 1989.

Bibliography

Beckett, Samuel. *Waiting for Godot*. New York: Grove Press, 1972.

Beckett, Samuel. *Endgame*. New York: Grove Press, 1958.

Beckett, Samuel. *Happy Days*. New York: Grove Press, 1961.

Bair, Deirdre. *Samuel Beckett*. New York: Harcourt Brace Jovanovich, 1978.

Ben-Zvi, Linda. *Samuel Beckett*. Boston: Twayne Publishers, 1986.

Godin, Georges and La Chance, Michaël. *Beckett, Entre le refus de l'art et le parcours mystique*. Canada: Le Castor Astral, 1994.

Gordon, Lois. *The World of Samuel Beckett 1906-1946*. New Haven: Yale University Press, 1996.

Simon, Alfred. *Samuel Beckett*. Paris: Pierre Belfond, 1983.

---

[36] Pozzo is a protagonist of *Waiting for Godot* 54.

[37] Clov is a protagonist of *Endgame* 27.

What is Irony?

This publication does not intend to reconstruct the meaning of Samuel Beckett's drama but to catch a glimpse of it through the lens of irony. With this purpose in mind, the chapter "What is irony?" presents a theoretical framework that will be used to analyze Samuel Beckett's dramatic trilogy: *Waiting for Godot, The Endgame* and *Happy Days*. I feel profoundly indebted to the critics that I cite, particularly with Soren Kierkegaard, Wayne Booth and Northrop Frye. Their respective contributions *The Concept of Irony, With Constant Reference to Socrates, A Rhetoric of Irony* and *Anatomy of Criticism* provide the grid with whitch the scenes and dramatic effects of Beckett's drama will be measured.[1]

I do not imply that the rest of the works cited in this publication occupy a lower level on the theoretical framework of irony. On the contrary, it's the cumulative effect of the distinct approaches that provide the

---

[1] Soren Kierkegaard. *The Concept of Irony, With Constant Reference to S crates* (Bloomington: Indiana University Press, 1968) Trans. Lee M. Capel.

Wayne C. Booth. *A Rhetoric of Irony* (Chicago: University of Chicago Press, 1974)

Northrop Frye. *Anatomy of Criticism, Four Essays* (New York: Atheneum, 1968)

critical umbrella under which this book seeks to encompass Beckett's dramatic trilogy.

I would like to add that most works that I cite have an implicit tendency to be applied to prose and poetry. Nonetheless, I have a hunch that Samuel Beckett's drama represents equally fertile grounds for ironic analysis. This publication should show that the plays have a great potential for ironic manifestations thanks to the three-dimensionality of their representation that couples the linguistic expression with esthetic and thematic attributes of the stage.

Plato and Socrates

If one linguistic term could represent irony, it would be *eirôneia*. Its almost regular appearance in an impressive diversity of critical analysis, commentaries and definitions suggests that the philosophers and critics try to define irony placing it in the time and *milieu* of Plato's epoch. The placement of irony's origin into the period of Early Greek Comedy or into Plato's citations gives a relatively stable meaning to the volatile concept of irony.[2] The significant and its signifier, such as they were used in Plato's time, remain relatively sheltered from transformations and diverse uses that the term sustained during following centuries even though there are contentious discussions about their correct translation

---

[2] Peter J. Roster. La ironía como método de análisis literario: la poesía de Salvador Novo (Madrid: Gredos, 1978) 11.

Philip Vellacott. Ironic drama (London: Cambridge University Press, 1975) 23.

Booth 23-130.

and interpretation. Plato used the term *eirôneia* to refer to witty Socrates who feigned ignorance during his philosophical discussions.[3]

The significance of *eirôneia*, during its first stage of formation and use, is based on the superposition of the two layers of meaning, wisdom and ignorance, that Socrates blended together.[4] In this context, ignorance hides, or tries to hide, wisdom. Nevertheless, the Greek people unmasked Socrates' ruse and overwhelmed him with praise and admiration.[5] I suspect that at this providential moment sparks the dynamic interplay between hiding and telling in the codification of irony. We shall see in the subsequent parts of this chapter how the original use of *eirôneia* evolved and ramified; but the polyvalent communicative link between Socrates and his people sets the foundation for irony that still holds true nowadays.

Kierkegaard

Kierkegaard's colossal study of irony represents the key abatement of the philosophical bridge that spans from the original use of *eirôneia* in Early Greek Comedy to its diverse meanings in the twentieth and twenty-first centuries. *The Concept of Irony, With Constant Reference to Socrates,* published in 1841, serves as the philosophical melting pot for different

---

[3] Vellacott 23.

[4] See:

Linda Hutcheon. "Ironía, sátira, parodia. Una aproximación pragmática a la ironía", *De la Ironía a lo grotesco*. Ed. Hernán Silva (Mexico: Universidad Metropolitana Iztapalapa, 1992) 177.

Frye 62.

Roster 11.

[5] Fabio Quintiliano. *Instituto oratorio* (Madrid: Hernando, 1942) Trans. Ignacio Rodríguez and Pedro Sandier, Vol. II, 100-1.

types of irony. In its crucible, original and modern concepts of *eirôneia* blend.

Analyzing the works of Socrates, Schlegel, Tieck, Schubert, Hegel and other writers and philosophers, Kierkegaard elaborates the concept of irony based on liberty and cancellation. The ironic subject or person cancels the limits imposed by reality for the sake of freedom that is experienced in the artistic or philosophical creation of the new realm. The theoretical relation between irony and freedom encompasses the second part of *The Concept of Irony, With Constant Reference to Socrates* in which Kierkegaard elaborates the theme of liberation on the social, metaphysical and linguistic levels. He pays close attention to the relation between reality and linguistics, as well as matter and poetics.[6]

Kierkegaard's contribution opens doors for modern readers and critics to whom he suggests to approach irony by canceling undesirable elements of the outside world.

> It is essential for the subject to become conscious of his irony, to feel negatively free when he condemns the given actuality and to enjoy this negative freedom. [...] When subjectivity asserts itself, irony appears.[7]

The three concepts mentioned in the previous citation -the disparity between reality and subjectivity, the ironist's subjectivity and the consciousness of being ironic- represent the fundamental base of the numerous, contemporary elaborations of irony.

Wayne Booth, probably the most read critic of irony in the twentieth century in North America and Europe, makes a commentary in the be-

---

[6] The roots of Kierkegaard's concept stem from the classical Greek literature, as well as from the romantic and philosophical works.
[7] Kierkegaard 280.

ginning of his work, *A Rhetoric of Irony*, on *The Concept of Irony, With Constant Reference to Socrates.*

> Kierkegaard's *The Concept of Irony* is to me one of the most interesting and profitable books ever written on an abstract idea -one of the very few books about Ideas which are not only delightful to read but from which one actually learns something. It is such a rich work that I cannot now state precisely where its influence leaves off and that of others begins.[8]

After a glorious praise of Kierkegaard's book that I cited in its minimal part, Booth declares in the continuation of the same passage: "Nothing he [Kierkegaard] says is of any use to me".[9] This contradiction will never cease to confound me. Aren't Kierkegaard's views on the disparity between the reality and subjectivity -as well as between the subjectivity of the ironist and his consciousness of being ironic- the fundamental ideas that occupy the first three chapters of *A Rhetoric of Irony*? In addition, it seems that Booth's gradual acceptance of the need to take into consideration the life of the author in order to interpret a text might have been inspired by one of his favorite writers: Kierkegaard.

Even the structure of *A Rhetoric of Irony*, in which the author exposes meticulously the elaboration of the theoretical framework and its application to literary analysis, could have been inspired subliminally by Kierkegaard's comments about the need to examine the process that led to a specific concept: "Everyone who has a result merely as such does not possess it, for he has not the way."[10] Booth might have conceived these ideas during his meticulous and abundant readings or through his

---

[8] Booth xiii.
[9] Booth xiii.
[10] Kierkegaard 340.

individual meditations but I believe it is worthwhile mentioning the simi-
larities in structure and content between *A Rhetoric of Irony* and Kierkegaard's publication *The Concept of Irony, With Constant Reference to
Socrates*. This relation is maybe validated by Booth himself, who places
his analysis of Kierkegaard's work in the first place of the long list of
philosophers whom he studied. He also dedicates to Kierkegaard a dis-
proportionally long praise in comparison to other writers. These coincidences, among many others, are an example of the ironic construction as
one reads Booth's declaration that nothing Kierkegaard says is of any use
to him.[11]

Kierkegaard's irony has universal dimensions as his concepts of infinity and totality are deeply rooted in Hegel's and Schubert's works.
Kierkegaard was fascinated by Schubert's *Symbolik des Traumes* in
which universal applications of irony are manifested.[12] Besides the universal infinity that Schubert explores as the domain of ironic investigation, the universe shows according to Kierkegaard that the ironic
objectivity does not exist in nature. Irony needs to be unveiled with subjective analysis: "All such [ironic] features are not in nature, but the
ironic subject perceives them in nature."[13] Schubert's concepts of univer-
sality and subjectivity contribute to the gestation of Kierkegaard's
thought and to the works of such twentieth-century critics and philosophers as Linda Hutcheon, Charles Irving Glicksberg, Douglas Colin
Muecke, etc.

The structure of *The Concept of Irony, With Constant Reference to
Socrates* is strongly influenced by the subjacent presence of Christian
morality that gives an additional dimension to irony. As it often occurs in
life and thus in philosophy, the application of a new and enriching con-

---

[11]   Booth xiii.
[12]   Schubert. *Symbolik des Traumes* (Bamberg, 1821).
[13]   Kierkegaard 272.

cept implies negation. Kierkegaard contends: "It is necessary to negate (or cancel) in order to affirm (or create)". Basing his philosophical thought on this principle, Kierkegaard asserts that Schlegel's and Solger's philosophies are morally negative and consequently defines the true morality in his publication.[14]

Modern Critics

Linda Hutcheon proposes in her study of irony the separation between "verbal" and "situational" ironies.[15] Hutcheon explains that the former refers to relatively short segments in which a semantic inversion occurs. In her example, "And Brutus is an honorable man", the semantic value arises from the "antiphrasis".[16] On the other hand, "situational irony" requires the consideration of the work's cumulative context. Hutcheon also elaborates "evaluative intention" that is based on the "author-encoder" and the knowledge of the "reader-receptor".[17] The author of the irony expects an analytical effort from the reader, and the subsequent bond between the two is established metaphysically. Both sides need to establish a link of complicity in order for the irony to crystallize.[18]

In his analysis of Hume's work, John Vladimir Price refers to Hutcheon's concept of "situational irony" as "ironic tone".[19] The purpose of

---

[14] Kierkegaard 308-11, 327.

[15] Hutcheon 173.

[16] Catherine Kerbrat-Orecchioni. "La ironía como tropo", *De la Ironía a lo grotesco*. Ed. Hernán Silva (Mexico: Universidad Metropolitana Iztapalapa, 1992) 195-7. Trans. Pilar Hernández Cobos.

[17] Hutcheon 175.

[18] Kierkegaard 273.

[19] John Vladimir Price. *The Ironic Hume* (Austin: University of Texas Press, 1965) 6-9.

the ironic tone is to express the cumulative effect of different messages: "The ironic tone is, in a familiar phrase, greater than the sum total of its various parts."[20] Price shows that Hume's ironic tone is not only an esthetic element but a cumulative thematic compound that defines the structure of his work.

The ironic tone expresses Hume's polemic points of view thanks to "artificial tolerance".[21] This concept has a double function: it protects and communicates. The "artificial tolerance" protects the ironist and it permits him to send an encoded message.

In the first section of *A Rhetoric of Irony*, which is based on "stable irony"[22], Booth elaborates a highly applicable concept of irony that could be used to analyze different types of irony. On various occasions, the author emphasizes the need for a sensitive reader to detect irony[23]. Even though absolute certainty in the interpretation of an irony does not exist, the concept of a stable irony implies a satisfactory level of certainty in interpretation that should allow the reader to establish and maintain the significance of an irony throughout the text. Catherine Kerbrat refers to this significance as "derived"[24], while Booth emphatically points out that the stability or certainty of an irony is ironic as it is based on the subjective interpretation of the reader.[25] In Booth's definition of stable irony, the following steps may be used as guidelines:

---

[20] Price 7.
[21] Price 5.
[22] Booth 23-130.
[23] Booth 1, 25 and 86.
[24] Kerbrat-Orecchioni 198.
[25] Booth 131-292.

1. The message should be intentionally created. In other words, the intention of sending an ironic message should exist during the codification process.[26]

2. The meaning of an ironic message needs to be "covert".[27] The message must have two distinct interpretations so that one can conceal the other. John Fletcher complements Booth's point of view with respect to the codification of the message and uses Samuel Beckett's writing as an example.[28] According to Fletcher, Beckett masks his personal suffering with "erudite but not necessarily obscure language".[29] As an example of the two levels of meaning and Beckett's tendency to hide his suffering, Fletcher mentions the author's use of Latin:

> he plants a quotation from Dante's *Infierno*: "secret things" is a translation of *secret cose*, Dante's expression for the shameful arcane of Hell to which his alter ego is about to be introduced by Virgil (*Infierno*, III, 21).[30]

3. During the analysis of a *stable* irony, the reader can assume that the first interpretation of the ironic message is correct. He does not need to undermine or keep deconstructing and reconstructing the ironic message to come up with a meaning. The tendency to stop the interpretative process could be seen as a sign of stable irony, while the continuous search reflects an unstable irony.

---

[26] In the second half of Booth's book, some examples of irony are based on haphazard or coincidences and not on the author's intentions.

[27] Booth 31.
Similar concept: Kerbrat-Orecchioni 198.

[28] John Fletcher. "Beckett as Poet", *Samuel Beckett: a collection of criticism.* Ed. Ruby Cohn (New York: McGraw-Hill Book Company, 1975) 42-4.

[29] Fletcher 43.

[30] Fletcher 43.

These steps have been analyzed from several points of view in *A Rhetoric of Irony* and they represent a valuable reference in the formation and interpretation of irony. Booth's work adds a new dimension to the search for the limits of the ironic interpretation which he presented as one of the major goals of his analysis: How can the relationship between the author and the reader of an ironic passage be defined? The doubt concerning the codification and decoding of the ironic message is intensified in the second part of *A Rhetoric of Irony*, in which the author's attention is focused on the search for meanings that are constantly more remote.[31] In the fourth chapter, Booth analyses ironies whose meaning is unlimited or unstable and absolutely subjective.[32] Thus, his work covers the entire horizon of possible interpretations, while the narrator invites the reader to follow the progressive analysis during which his thought ripens and spans the chasm between two extremes: objective and subjective ironies.

Peter Roster's definition and analysis of irony are rhetorically and figuratively based on the "system rupture".[33] The formation of the ironic message according to Roster's theory surges from the author's disillusion. The author realizes that there is a discrepancy between the ideal and real worlds, appearance and reality, etc.[34] Sharing his disillusion with the reader, the ironic author opens the abyss or "rupture" between contrasting sides. His posture is distinct from Booth's theoretical framework, which is based on differential nuances and tacit suggestions.

---

[31]   Booth 293-312.
[32]   Booth 313-344.
[33]   Roster 17.
[34]   Roster 17.

Transformations of Booth's Irony

In the initial references to the "author" in *A Rhetoric of Irony*, Booth gives the privileged place to the implicit author in comparison to the author-writer. The author-writer remains outside of the initial, theoretical framework of Booth's theory just as it is often omitted in modern, literary criticism.[35]

> Our best evidence of the intentions behind any sentence in *Candide* will be the whole of *Candide*, and for some critical purposes it thus makes sense to talk only of the *work*'s intentions, not the author's.[36]

But in the third chapter of the first part of *A Rhetoric of Irony*, "Is it ironic?", Booth contemplates the elements related to the life as well as to the personal and literary characteristics or the author.

> Can I [...] make all necessary inferences about the implied author's norms on the basis of the text itself [...] or must I [...] search for 'external' clues about the author's probable intentions?[37]

When confronted by widespread ambiguities of irony in the second part of his book, Booth starts using extrinsic information in order to find adequate interpretations. He concludes that the reader should pay close attention to the writer's style and objectives.

---

[35] In chapters three, four and five, my analysis of Samuel Beckett's plays is also devoid of references to the author. The ties between the author and his work are sketched in the first chapter and the conclusion of this book.

[36] Booth 11.

[37] Booth 53.

The use of the knowledge about Flannery O'Connor's life and work shores up Booth's deductions.[38] In the analysis of *Everything that goes up has to come down*, the information about the life and work of O'Connor is essential for Booth's interpretations as he affirms:

> But those of us who have read many of Flannery O'Connor's stories and studied her life will be unable to resist seeing Julian's final problematic redemption as presented in a religious light, even a specifically Roman Catholic light [...][39]

There is no doubt that Booth guides us consciously through the gradual crystallization of his theory. One could even say that the reader is the privileged witness of Booth's mental gestation from which springs his theoretical framework. The sequence of questions that the author addresses to the reader shows the collaborative link between Booth and the reader. The advantage of Booth's theoretical elaboration, in comparison with the mere presentation of the final conclusions, stems from the reader's intellectual pleasure and involvement in the interpretative process. The text invites the reader to participate in the construction of the theoretical framework and thus the reader becomes a part of it.

As aforementioned, Booth explicitly states that the difference between stable and unstable ironies depends on the degree of certainty in the ironic decoding. On the other hand, if the terms express the irony with absolute certainty, they eliminate the ironic effect.[40] Linda Hutcheon also describes the inverse relation between the number of signs and irony's effect.

---

[38]   Booth 215-30.
[39]   Booth 167-8.
[40]   Booth 31.

[...] el grado de efecto irónico en un texto es inversamente proporcional al número de signos manifiestos necesarios para lograr este efecto.[41]

At the same time, Hutcheon indicates that without signs or indications the ironic communication can not be established:

[...] esos signos tienen que existir [...] para remitir al lector a la intención evaluativa codificada por el autor.[42]

The ironist faces an enigma as he needs to find a midpoint between insufficiency of signs, which would render the decoding impossible, and their superabundance, which would cancel irony.

The formula of the inverse proportion between the number of signs and the ironic effect sounds perfectly logical, but I thought about *Animal Farm* by George Orwell.[43] A multitude of critics from the four cardinal points have deduced that it is an ironic novel. Interpretations vary but often refer to: totalitarianism of one sort or another, abuse of power camouflaged with Marxist slogans, discrepancy between what is said and done[44], etc. It would be difficult to find a reader who has trouble grasping the ironic tone of the novel because of the overwhelming number of signs and images that point in that direction. The ironic signs abound; every page is a new point of reference that complements the puzzle that

---

[41] Hutcheon 179.
[...] the degree of ironic effect in a text is inversely proportional to the number of signs necessary to create this effect. (my translation)
See also: Kerbrat-Orecchioni 198.
[42] Hutcheon 179.
[...] these signs have to exist [...] in order to show to the reader the author's intention. (my translation)
[43] George Orwell. *Animal Farm* (London: David Campbell, 1993)
[44] Richard Smyer. *Animal Farm: pastoralism and politics* (Boston: Twayne Publishers, 1988) 35.

was already decoded. Why then doesn't this abundance of signs diminish or cancel the ironic effect as Hutcheon and Booth suggest it would?

We find ourselves in a problematic situation; an almost universally accepted principle is questioned, even canceled by a well-known literary work. Could we say that George Orwell's literary genius has unintentionally toppled the premises of Linda Hutcheon, Wayne Booth, Douglas Colin Muecke and many other critics?[45] The only explanation that I can suggest is that the novel does not contain one irony but a multitude of ironies which compose a monumental puzzle in which each piece has a different form and nuance. *Animal Farm* is a series of diverse, ironic images that thanks to George Orwell's simple virtuosity entertain the reader and make him reflect upon human nature. The effectiveness of the ironic net is continuously reinforced with new ironic knots. These knots maintain the readers' attention focused on the narrative's turns and twists as the number of ironic images is limited only by Orwell's creative imagination.

Ironic Signs

When a reader senses an obvious error, conflict of facts or clashes of style in the text, Booth suggests that he/she examines the text skeptically in order to detect a possible irony.[46] The deformation of a popular expression can also be an attempt to involve the reader in the ironic game. The substitution of a fly by an airplane, in the statement "one could hear

---

[45]   Hutcheon 179.

Douglas Colin Muecke. *Irony and the ironic* (London: Methuen, 1982) 27.

[46]   Booth 47-86.

an airplane", is a clear indication that the reader should not take the information literally.

The contrasting information is also a sign of incoherence. The implicit author could have placed a false statement in the text or established a double irony. Booth borrows a segment from Muecke's text to give an example of double irony: "The penguins had the most powerful army in the world. So had the porpoises."[47] The presence of two incoherent statements indicates the presence of an unstable irony in which the objective points of reference remain beyond the reader's reach.

Vellacott, Roster, Frye, Kerbrat, Cohn and Others

Since the nineteenth century, numerous publications on irony have proliferated. In many cases, the names of new theories are distinct but their content remains within the parameters of preestablished concepts. Among these approaches, the dramatic and metaphysical ironies seem to be complementary and relevant to Samuel Beckett's drama.

Philip Vellacott bases the concept of dramatic irony on the protagonist's expectations, the unfolding of the play and the presence of the spectator as a witness.[48] Irony emerges from the emptiness that separates the protagonist's expectations from the imminent tragedy. The spectator realizes that the tragic ending awaits the protagonist but he continues to hope and strive for his salvation. The ironic intensity inches up due to the close relationship between the protagonist and the spectator. The dra-

---

[47] Booth 62.
[48] Vellacott 23-4.

matic thread is taught from the stage and the auditorium, as both sides are indispensable for the ironic bond.

Peter Roster studies the same concepts as Philip Vellacott but he emphasizes the impact of the spectator's disappointment or dissatisfaction.[49] Realizing that the protagonist is in dire straits, the spectator subconsciously expects a change in his behavior but it never occurs. The protagonist's progression toward his tragic end and the spectator's increasing anguish constitute the additional dimension in dramatic irony.

Northrop Frye elaborates the concept of "tragic irony" contributing two new elements to Peter Roster's and Philip Vellacott's theory: isolation and arbitrariness.[50] According to Frye, the staging of the tragic irony is situated in the isolation, which can be established gradually or instantaneously, and the punishment is inflicted upon the protagonist in an arbitrary manner as if the victim were selected haphazardly.[51] The incongruency and inevitability are combined in Frye's reconstruction of the tragic irony and he mentions Kafka's *Process* and Jesus Christ's life as examples.

Booth cites a passage from *Tartuffe* which is suitable *par excellence* for the analysis of dramatic irony thanks to Elmire's exaggerated search for certainty. Orgon, Elmire's husband, is hiding under the table and perfectly visible to the audience. Elmire allows Tartuffe, a courteous hypocrite, to unfold his seductive talents in order to finally show to her husband his true nature. The spectator gets impatient waiting for Orgon to respond vehemently to his guest's hypocrisy. In the meantime, Tartuffe manifests the utmost verbal dexterity in the defamation of his host:

---

[49] Roster 14.
[50] Frye 63-75.
[51] Frye 64.

Why worry about the man? Each day he grows
More gullible; one can lead him by the nose.
To find us here would fill him with delight,
And if he saw the worst, he'd doubt his sight.[52]

Confounded by her husband's silence or mental instability, Elmire forces him to come out of hiding once Orgon has left. Orgon crawls out clumsily and Elmire confronts him with some of the most amusing questions and comments:

What, coming out so soon? How premature!
Get back in hiding, and wait until you're sure.
Stay till the end, and be convinced completely;
We mustn't stop till things are proved concretely....
Wait, and be certain that there's no mistake.
No jumping to conclusions, for Heaven's sake! [IV, vi][53]

In this scene, the spectator can appreciate several aspects of dramatic irony. On the one hand, Tartuffe's hypocrisy coincides with the structure of irony; the appearance or the first impression of the guest does not correspond to his true nature. On the other, the spectator enjoys the dramatic representation of irony: "No jumping to conclusions..."[54] In this scene, the difference between the spectator's knowledge and the protagonist's ignorance fades away because Orgon finally learns who his guest is. The loss of the difference between their views contributes to their intimacy. Orgon's inquisitive nature is also representative of the reader's search for the presence and meaning of irony.

---

[52] Booth 66.
[53] Booth 67.
[54] Booth 67.

I found Charles Glicksberg's definition of metaphysical or general irony very pertinent to the study of Samuel Beckett's drama.[55] His theory is based on the incomprehensible contradictions in human existence. Metaphysical or general irony differs from dramatic irony as it focuses on the totality of human existence and not merely on one situation or an individual life. Glicksberg's theory seeks the transcendental significance of human life and manifests its incapacity to find it. The failure of this search leads to the conclusion that life is devoid of significance and causes the human being's fall into emptiness.[56] The intriguing aspect of this theory consists of the indefinite continuation of the search as if the impossibility of a successful conclusion were a catalyzer. This aspect of Glicksberg's theory finds a stunning echo in Beckett's plays, particularly in *Waiting for Godot* and *Endgame* as we shall see later in this study.

Alain Robbe-Grillet explains the continuous search with absurdity. The plot does not offer a logical justification for its existence, but the sole fact that the protagonists are on stage permits the play to proceed toward an imaginary end.

[...] but they remain riveted to these two beings who do nothing, say practically nothing, have no other property but that of being there.[57]

According to Allain Robbe-Grillet, the absence of a solution to the enigmatic questions about life precipitates the human being into the chaotic realm of the absurd.

---

[55] Charles Irving Glicksberg. *The ironic vision in modern literature* (The Hugue, Martinus Nijhoff, 1969) 43.

[56] Glicksberg 44.

[57] Alain Robbe-Grillet. "Samuel Beckett, or 'Presence' in the Theater", *S muel Beckett, A collection of critical essays.* Ed. Martin Esslin (New Jersey: Prentice Hall, 1965) 110.

Muecke characterizes metaphysical irony as inherent to the human condition that sentences the man/woman to an inevitable failure: "the ironist sees the whole of mankind as victims".[58] Ruby Cohn also shares the view of the inevitable failure in the interpretation of Samuel Beckett's work: "[...] the art of failure, time's erosion of life, the inadequacy and even impossibility of love."[59] Cohn's and Muecke's definitions of metaphysical irony coincide in their interpretation of the ineluctable fall into emptiness and hopelessness.

In David Worcester's concept of cosmic irony, the reader finds out that human beings' analysis is always inferior to a superior "knowledge".[60] The human contemplation of life and existence reflects a vain effort to penetrate into the realm of true knowledge. Maurice Nadeau describes the human condition in Samuel Beckett's and Franz Kafka's works in light of the theories that we have seen: "Nothing is certain but the void, and error, and the idiotic race which every man seems condemned to run to no purpose [...]"[61] The term "idiotic race" depicts the absurd search whose end, if it exists, is doomed to failure.

Price interprets Hume's view as an act of resignation when faced with human destiny. His description of Hume's work is similar to Maurice Nadeau's exploration of Samuel Beckett's and Franz Kafka's literary and dramatic contributions. Price asserts that "Hume morosely feared that many problems in philosophy, in ethics, and in human behavior were

---

[58] Roster 16.

[59] Ruby Cohn. "Inexhaustible Beckett: An Introduction", *Samuel Beckett: a collection of criticism*. Ed. Ruby Cohn (New York: McGraw-Hill Book Company, 1975) 1.

[60] David Worcester. *The Art of Satire* (New York: Norton, 1969) 132.

[61] Maurice Nadeau. "Samuel Beckett: Humor and the Void", *Samuel Beckett, A collection of critical essays*. Ed. Martin Esslin (New Jersey: Prentice Hall, 1965) 34.

insoluble."[62] Hume's skepticism and resignation, similar to those of Samuel Beckett, are not an impediment for the literary creation but a lens through which the writer sees humankind.

Peter Roster makes a valuable contribution to the theoretical elaboration of cosmic and philosophical ironies. He shows that the message sent to the reader or spectator does not include the description of the cause that leads the protagonists to the state of despair and isolation.[63] The cause of their plight is absent but its effects are present in the text or dramatic representation.

In Roster's work, the nature of the presence or absence of the cosmic cause for human despair is analogous to Catherine Kerbrat-Orecchioni's definition of irony. Kerbrat, like Booth, specifies that the signs of irony need to be *in absentia* in order for the decoding process to unfold adequately: "La ironía no puede existir legítimamente más que en la ausencia de índices demasiado insistentes."[64] The undefined cause of the metaphysical or cosmic irony and the absence of ironic signs, described respectively by Roster and Kerbrat-Orecchioni, form a mystical realm in which Samuel Beckett's drama takes place. The absence of the cause is a crucial ingredient in the formation of the subjective world that places Beckett's drama into the domain of unstable irony.

Frye's and Kerbrat-Orecchioni's study of the definite article seems to contradict *a priori* the significance of an element *in absentia*[65] because it *overtly* indicates the presence of a covert communication among the

---

[62] Price 9.

[63] Roster 28-9.

[64] Kerbrat-Orecchioni 196-7.
    Irony can exist legitimately only in the absence of ostentatious signs. (my translation)

[65] Kerbrat-Orecchioni 196.
    Frye 98.

members of a group.[66] Behind the obvious significance of the message lies a codified message that can be detected, thanks to the definite article, by the individuals who share the secrets of the group. The fact that the article is definite indicates that the significance is known to those who are involved in the communication even though its meaning is not explicitly stated.[67] Thus, the definite article indicates the presence and at the same time the absence of a message.

Problematic Effect of Irony

In this chapter, we have seen some characteristics of irony but very little about its effects on the individual who decodes it. Peter Roster presents various concepts related to the effects of irony in *La ironía como método de análisis literario: la poesía de Salvador Novo*:

> Esta reacción [a la ironía] la podemos caracterizar como una sensación agridulce que no rinde al lector ni una satisfacción ni una descarga c mpletas. Los factores principales que explican esta reacción son la simpatía o identificación que el lector siente con la víctima (o el acuerdo con la justicia del sentimiento expresado en la ironía) y la sensación que -aunque subconsciente- siente de haber sido engañado por el ironista.[68]

---

[66] Frye 99.

[67] Worth uses the concept of absence in the analysis of formal esthetics of Samuel Beckett's drama:
Katherine Worth. "The space and the sound in Beckett's theater", *Beckett the shape changer*. Ed. Katherine Worth (London: Routledge & Kegan Paul, 1975) 185-7.

[68] Roster 35.

The bittersweet or "painfully comical" aspect is usually well accepted by critics of irony.[69] Both aspects, painful and comical, may min-
gle in the decoder's mind but Peter Roster's assertion that the satisfaction
and catharsis are absent in the ironic interpretation seem erroneous to me.
Roster affirms that the lack of satisfaction and catharsis is caused by the
sympathy or identification of the decoder with the victim. The victim
cannot feel the catharsis because his feelings were hurt in the process of
being tricked. From my point of view, both the ironist and the reader or
spectator feel a great satisfaction when completing the circle of ironic
communication. In other words, they feel involved in the tacit communication that establishes personal ties between the author and the reader or
between the dramatic character and the spectator. To be initially tricked
and to discover *a posteriori* the implicit message is not an impediment
for the satisfaction but a path toward it.

It is true, as Roster states, that after some ironic messages the decoder is left with a bitter or unpleasant feeling because he identified himself with the victim. However, this bitterness does not prevent the
catharsis that the irony generates. The readers of *Candide* by Voltaire or
A Modest Proposal by Jonathan Swift experience a tremendous relief
despite the pain that the destiny has inflicted on the protagonists. The
archetypal case of Œdipus reveals the complementarity between the
spectator's catharsis and his *pathos* for the protagonist. The relief experienced at the end of this play would not take the form of laughter but of a

---

We can describe this reaction [to irony] as a bittersweet sensation that
does not offer any satisfaction or a complete catharsis to the reader. The major
elements that explain this reaction are affection or identification that the reader
feels for the victim (or the agreement with the validity of the expressed feeling
in the irony) and the sentiment that he/she feels -even subconsciously- that
he/she has been tricked by the ironist.

[69]   Muecke 51.

catharsis induced by the ironic destiny of the protagonist who was unable to "see" until he became blind.

* * *

In this chapter, we saw some major characteristics of irony, while keeping in mind the stylistic and thematic profile of Samuel Beckett's work. Wayne Booth's method for the identification of irony, Philip Vellacott's view of the spectator as a witness, Kierkegaard's search for freedom through the ironic negation and other approaches to irony guided me in the analysis of Samuel Beckett's drama from an ironic perspective.[70]

Bibliography

Booth, Wayne C. *A Rhetoric of Irony.* Chicago: University of Chicago Press, 1974.

Cohn, Ruby. "Inexhaustible Beckett: An Introduction". *Samuel Beckett: a collection of criticism.* Ed. Ruby Cohn. New York: McGraw-Hill Book Company, 1975.

Fletcher, John. "Beckett as Poet". *Samuel Beckett: a collection of criticism.* Ed. Ruby Cohn. New York: McGraw-Hill Book Company, 1975.

Frye, Northrop. *Anatomy of Criticism, Four Essays.* New York: Atheneum, 1968.

Glicksberg, Charles Irving. *The ironic vision in modern literature.* The Hugue: Martinus Nijhoff, 1969.

---

[70] Booth 90-104.
Vellacott 23.

Hutcheon, Linda. "Ironía, sátira, parodia. Una aproximación pragmática a la ironía". *De la Ironía a lo grotesco*. Ed. Hernán Silva. Mexico: Universidad Metropolitana Iztapalapa, 1992. Trans. Pilar Hernández Cobos.

Kerbrat-Orecchioni, Catherine. "La ironía como tropo". *De la Ionía a lo grotesco*. Ed. Hernán Silva. Mexico: Universidad Metropolitana Iztapalapa, 1992. 195-221. Trans. Pilar Hernández Cobos.

Kierkegaard, Soren. *The concept of Irony, With Constant Reference to Socrates*. Bloomington: Indiana University Press, 1968. Trans. Lee M. Capel.

Muecke, Douglas Colin. *Irony and the ironic*. London: Methuen, 1982.

Nadeau, Maurice. "Samuel Beckett: Humor and the Void". *Samuel Beckett, A collection of critical essays*. Ed. Martin Esslin. New Jersey: Prentice Hall, 1965. 33-36.

Orwell, George. *Animal farm*. London: David Campbell, 1993.

Price, John Vladimir. *The Ironic Hume*. Austin: University of Texas Press, 1965.

Quintiliano, Fabio. *Insituto oratorio*. Madrid: Hernando, 1942. Trans. Ignacio Rodríguez and Pedro Sandier.

Robbe-Grillet, Alain. "Samuel Beckett, or 'Presence' in the Theater". *Samuel Beckett, A collection of critical essays*. Ed. Martin Esslin. New Jersey: Prentice Hall, 1965.

Roster, Peter J. *La ironía como método de análisis literario: la poesía de Salvador Novo*. Madrid: Gredos, 1978.

Smyer, Richard. *Animal farm: pastoralism and politics*. Boston: Twayne Publishers, 1988.

Vellacott, Philip. *Ironic drama*. London: Cambridge University Press, 1975.

Worcester, David. *The Art of Satire*. New York: Norton, 1969.

Worth, Katherine. "The space and the sound in Beckett's theater". *Beckett the shape changer*. Ed. Katherine Worth. London: Routledge & Kegan Paul, 1975. 185-218.

Ironic Games in *Waiting for Godot*

The initial information about the play is communicated to the spectator through its title: *Waiting for Godot*. This information might be essential for the interpretation of the play as it precedes its viewing. For this hypothesis to be true, one must assume that the spectator knows the title of the play before seeing it. Nevertheless, the information contained in the title could be misleading. The spectator seated in the Théâtre de Babylone during *Waiting for Godot*'s première in 1952 and millions of other spectators that saw it during the following years were tricked or at least misled by the play's title. The purpose of this chapter is to show that Godot's arrival is as ironic as the play's title. The identity of Godot is so tightly interwoven with ambiguous suppositions that it questions not only his arrival but his very existence.

The dramatic situations and the protagonists' mental processes blend during ironic games. The protagonists' behavior and their interpersonal ties evolve during the representation manifesting their complementary and contradictory characteristics.[1] The comical aspects of their interac-

---

[1] Fernando de Toro shows how scenic elements are integrated into the representation:

tion do not blot out the existential drama but provide it with a ludic appearance.[2]

Time and Space

In the opening scenes, spectators observe the protagonists' futile activities such as taking off Estragon's boots, fighting for the handkerchief, playing with the hats, etc., which are followed by the commentaries about their boredom. The way actors absorb the spectator's attention is an enigma of Samuel Beckett's drama.[3] They are akin to marionettes suspended on invisible threads that entangle the spectator who peers at them. After some frustrating attempts to disentangle himself by smirking at the absurd situation and trifling activities, the spectator and the protagonists start anticipating Godot's arrival and hoping to resolve the play's conundrum.[4] As the title suggests, waiting for Godot is the central

---

Fernando de Toro. "El discurso teatral", *Semiótica del teatro* (Carleton: Editorial Galerna, 1994) 26-31.

[2] Roster studies contrasts, such as "appearance vs. reality":

Peter J. Roster. *La ironía como método de análisis literario: la poesía de Salvador Novo* (Madrid: Gredos, 1978) 17.

[3] Stanislavski and Wright show how the spectator identifies himself with the protagonist:

Constantin Stanislavski. *Un actor se prepara* (Mexico: Editorial Diana, 1994) 166.

Edward Wright. *Para comprender el teatro actual* (Mexico: Fondo de Cultura Económica, 1978) 29.

[4] Robbe-Grillet, Anders and Álvarez study the circular movement and esthetic aspects of time in Beckett's work:

Allain Robbe-Grillet. "Samuel Beckett, or 'Presence' in the Theater", *Samuel Beckett, A collection of critical essays.* Ed. Martin Esslin (New Jersey: Prentice Hall, 1965) 109.

theme of the play, which weighs heavily upon the protagonists and spectators.

The play starts taking ironic dimensions once the spectators try to define Godot and the circumstances related to his arrival. Despite spectators' analytical observations, Godot's profile remains shrouded in doubts. The irony in *Waiting for Godot* emerges from the incoherence between the protagonists' behavior and the general situation on stage. On the one hand, the protagonists dedicate themselves to waiting for Godot; and on the other, Godot's existence and arrival remain highly questionable. The total dedication to waiting for somebody whose time and place of arrival are undefined provides the bases for the situational irony:

> Estragon: You're sure it was here?
> Vladimir: What?
> Estragon: That we were to wait.
> Vladimir: He said by the tree. (*They look at the tree.*) Do you see any others? (10)

Estragon's question about the meeting place with Godot is answered by another question: "What?" Answering a question with a question plunges the protagonists and the spectator into a realm of hypothetical interpretations. The austere stage setting and the mound contribute to the illusion that the protagonists are adequately located to maximize the probability of seeing Godot. The emptiness that extends like a shadow toward the four cardinal points suggests that the protagonists are hemmed by a plane, while the mound hints that the protagonists are at the

---

Günther Anders. "Being without time: On Beckett's Play *Waiting for Godot*", *Samuel Beckett, A collection of critical essays*. Ed. Martin Esslin (New Jersey: Prentice Hall, 1965) 140.

A. Álvarez. *Samuel Beckett* (New York: Grove Press, 1961) 77.

best strategic position for the observation of the flat terrain. Thus, the spectator tentatively concludes that a trek to another spot would be a bad bet.

When Estragon forces Vladimir to observe the horizon in search of something or someone, Vladimir's effort reveals the protagonists' situation. With the back turned to the audience, Vladimir looks for human beings that could possibly be Godot and as the spectators are placed behind him Vladimir concludes that there is nobody in the proximity. The direction in which Vladimir looks represents the irony of his search. The shadows that surround him during his inspection of the terrain absorb and cancel his gaze just as the protagonists absorb the spectators' attention without revealing their identity. These observation attempts cancel each other, creating an aura of incomprehension around the protagonists and the spectator.[5] Vladimir's foggy view cannot but suggest a general state of confusion on stage.

The road that passes by the protagonists' camping grounds invites them to lift the camp and trek away. The road is not desolated because nobody is using it but because it does not have the capacity to jolt the protagonists out of their lethargy and motivate them to initiate a trip. Estragon's and Vladimir's life paths reflect the still and dull dirt road that is incapable of fomenting hope or motion.

The dramatic function of the tree, around which the protagonists are seated, is polyvalent. On the one hand, it incites the impulse of death: "What about hanging ourselves?" (12) On some occasions, the rope is missing; and on others, the motivation. Nonetheless, the tree points continuously in the direction of the suicide. On the other hand, the tree

---

[5] Wellershoff elaborates the paradigm of the permanent failure:
Dieter Wellershoff. "Failure of an Attempt at De-Mythologization: Samuel Beckett's Novels", *Samuel Beckett, A collection of critical essays*. Ed. Martin Esslin (New Jersey: Prentice Hall, 1965) 92.

represents a significant point of reference thanks to which Vladimir convinces Estragon that they are at the adequate location for the meeting with Godot: "He said by the tree. Do you see any others?" (10) The fact that it is the only tree in the vicinity implies that they are at the right spot and doing the right thing: waiting for Godot.

The false hope that the tree inspires coincides with the suicidal impulse that it exacerbates.[6] The tree ironically inspires both hope and suicide. It exercises a centripetal pull on both protagonists as if they were attached to the tree by a bond of life and death. As the representation inches toward its closure, the sinister aspect of the tree is reflected in Vladimir's enunciation: "Everything's dead but the tree". (59b) The tree's life contrasts Estragon's and Vladimir's hopeless waiting. If the spectator held onto a thread of hope regarding Godot's arrival during the initial stages of the play, at its closure, the desolation claims the dramatic space.

The road and the tree form a dramatic alliance which initially suggests the presence of human beings and the place of the meeting with Godot; but the two scenic elements prove to be misleading. The continuous announcements of Godot's arrival and his subsequent absence contribute to the transformation of the protagonists' situation. They start discussing the option of a suicide with increasing frequency. The restlessness does not cancel the waiting but it diminishes the hope of seeing Godot and thus prolongs *ad infinitum* the protagonists' suffering. Ironically, the most ostentatious scenic elements, the road and the tree, that

---

[6] Kerbrat-Orecchioni shows how contradictory aspects of a word or character blend together in an ironic context:

Catherine Kerbrat-Orecchioni. "La ironía como tropo", *De la Ironía a lo grotesco*. Ed. Hernán Silva (Mexico: Universidad Metropolitana Iztapalapa, 1992. Trans. Pilar Hernández Cobos) 196-7.

define the place of the meeting with Godot and inspire the hope of witnessing his arrival actually perpetuate the protagonists' suffering.

Need to Act

The protagonists' lack of determination does not cancel their acting as it represents the fundamental part of drama. A play without acting[7] has never been staged as its hypothetical performance would be a mere exhibition of actors. A play needs acting in order to fill the dramatic space and thus come to exist. Beckett managed to recreate the dramatic ambiance without words but not without acting, even though acting was reduced on one occasion to mere facial movements.

At least up to the beginning of the 21st century, acting has been an indispensable feature for the dramatic performance. In *Waiting for Godot*, Vladimir's and Estragon's *modus vivendi* not only fulfills the acting prerequisite for a dramatic performance but it also reflects the ironic hope of finding a solution to their plight. The loss of pragmatism in their role playing emphasizes their desperate waiting.

The acting on Beckett's stage is also a way to confirm the existence of protagonists whose logic and energy wane as the performance goes on. Through the continuous interaction, Vladimir and Estragon cancel, or at least postpone, the suicide and thus extend the thread of life pretending to comply with the rules of a game. The fragile imbalance that favors life is preserved thanks to the lack of motivation to commit suicide but the lack of motivation prevents them from leaving the tree and the mound. The protagonists' state of mind tips alternately the scale in opposite directions, toward life and death. If the scale were tipped excessively, fa-

---

[7] "Acting" in this sense refers to an actor's physical presence and role.

voring life or death, the change would mark the conclusion of the performance and it would be incoherent with the central axis of the play: the continuous waiting despite the hopelessness of the situation.

The protagonists' acting under dire conditions is revealed under the guise of a childish game. In the nightmarish context, a trace of agony tinges their ludic game.

> Estragon: This is how it is. (*He reflects.*) The bough... the bough... (*Angrily.*) Use your head, can't you?
> Vladimir: You're my only hope.
> Estragon: (*with effort*). Gogo light-bough not break-Gogo dead. Didi heavy-bough break-Didi alone. (12b)

The protagonists seek refuge in the state of infantile mentality in order to evade the harsh reality, but a suicide wish lurks behind their playful tone of voice. In brief fragments, resembling the poem of a child who is learning to versify, the sounds "di" and "go" that compose the protagonists' nicknames: Didi and Gogo. (12b) In an act of phonic fusion, their names form the term "dodo". French children use this word to refer to "sleep"; and the depth of the sleep can only be fathomed by Vladimir and Estragon.

Tiptoeing along the edge of an abyss while playing versifying games, the protagonists fall into their own trap. The joyful echoes of their names are coupled with the ominous content of their verses: "Gogo light-bough not break-Gogo dead." (12b). Even the double meaning of Vladimir's apparently innocent statement, "Use your head, can't you?" (12b), could suggest to Estragon to put his head through the rope's loop.

In the context of phonetic coincidences, the sounds of the nicknames "Gogo" and "Didi" also compose the name of their purported savior "Godot". Would it be an extension of the linguistic coincidence that Godot is the product of their imagination just as his name is the acoustic combination of their nicknames, Gogo and Didi?

Collective Games

The protagonists' games get diversified with the arrival of Lucky and Pozzo. Lucky introduces himself with the performance of awkward movements and invites Estragon to imitate him. Estragon attempts the eccentric performance but after a few errors abandons the feat: "With a little practice." (26b) The improvised competition between the protagonists and their subsequent discussion about the dance create the illusion of an incipient social link between the two groups. The impossibility to form a truly interactive unit and take a collective decision to remain by the tree or take the road reveals the superficiality of their union. The words and movements that muster their attention evaporate as soon as the game is over.

Even though Estragon and Vladimir can not come to a clear conclusion about their situation, Estragon reveals it unconsciously by dubbing Lucky's dance: "The Scapegoat's Agony." (27) The name of the dance manifests its dramatic intensity through spontaneity and simplicity. It is direct and precise because it is free of tension that the protagonists feel when they speak about their future or Godot's arrival. The coincidence between Vladimir's and Estragon's mental state and the nature of Lucky's dance permits them to describe spontaneously the panorama of their situation[8]: «The Scapegoat's Agony».

---

[8] Stanislavski and Bentley explore characters' and spectators' psychological aspects, and show how they contribute to the staging of a play from the actor's and spectator's points of view:

Vladimir's and Estragon's trying on of the hats gives the impression to the spectator that he is facing two mentally retarded persons or toddlers. Generally, the audience is silent during the performance unless a child has been sneaked in. A child's laughter or giggle might show his or her identification with the protagonists' game.

The scene with the hats and the imitation of Pozzo and Lucky introduce the problematic concept of Vladimir's and Estragon's identity. Usurping others' place, Vladimir and Estragon feel a gratifying sensation of relief.

> Vladimir: I'll do Lucky, you do Pozzo. (*He imitates Lucky sagging under the weight of his baggage. Estragon looks at him with stupefaction.*) Go on.
> Estragon: What am I to do?
> Vladimir: Curse me! (47)

It is curious that Vladimir feels euphoric pretending to carry Lucky's load but, on the other hand, everything is preferable to his own plight. Even though Lucky's burden is hefty, it does not bear any existential thorns. As Vladimir sags imitating Lucky, he brings to mind the archetypal image of Sisyphus and at the same time reflects the comical image of Charles Chaplin. Either role provides the protagonist with a task that camouflages his situation.

Besides the fact that Vladimir does not really feel Lucky's burden and only uses its esthetic aspects, Vladimir can interrupt his drudgery whenever he wishes. Thus, the imitation of Lucky and Pozzo has a triple beneficial effect. First, the game allows them to postpone at least temporarily the burden of their own existence; second, they enjoy the ludic

---

Stanislavski 237.

E. Bentley. *La vida del drama* (Mexico: Paidos Studio, 1982) 61.

aspects of the mimicking farce; and third, they enjoy the power of being able to interrupt the game at any time, unlike their real game.

The protagonists' imitation of Lucky and Pozzo opens doors to dramatic irony. By adopting the roles of their counterparts, Vladimir and Estragon experience an amnesia that cancels the reality and they feel an ethereal sensation of happiness. Pretending to be blind, Vladimir loses sight of Estragon; and when Vladimir regains his vision, he seems to be euphoric about the encounter with the old friend: "There you are again at last." (47) As if the protagonist were implementing a mathematical formula in which two signs of negation, represented by the suffering of the two groups, cancel each other and set the stage for illusions.[9]

In the context of tragi-comical games, the protagonists undertake the search for the solution in the cavities of their boots and hats. During the presentation, Vladimir specializes in the analysis of his hat and Estragon in the observation of his boots. Both look intently into these cavities as if they wanted to combine the surrounding desolation with the emptiness of their garments.

The protagonists' puzzling search is so contagious that the spectator might get surprised by the wavering expectation in his own mind to find the answer to Vladimir's and Estragon's problematic existence in the places where the good sense, view and smell instinctively balk. The protagonists' search becomes the spectator's expectation.

In the opening scene of the second act, Estragon declares that the boots that he has left on stage in the previous act are not his: "They are not mine. [...] Mine were black. These are brown." (43b) The spectator is momentarily disoriented by Estragon's amnesia and tries to remember the exact color and shape of the boots, as well as the place where the

---

[9] See "incongruities" and "style contrasts":
Wayne C. Booth. *A Rhetoric of Irony* (Chicago: University of Chicago Press, 1974) 36 and 107.

protagonist left them before nightfall.[10] The spectator's doubt is the product of the protagonists' contagious mental instability. The illusions and doubts that are produced on stage overflow the stage planks and spill over into the orchestra pit. The mental and physical disorientation brings the two sides of the dramatic space together.

The Tree and the Amnesia

Besides serving as a topographic point of reference, the tree transforms and deconstructs the concept of time as its leaves grow in one night, defying laws of botany. If the spectator takes into consideration only the esthetic transformation of the tree, the ironic clues pass unnoticed. Nonetheless, the incapacity of the protagonists to change their situation offers a contrasting setting in comparison with the abrupt transformation of the tree. The stunning change in the tree's aspect and the protagonists' static existence submerge the spectator even deeper into the incomprehensible world of ironic laws.[11]

> Vladimir: But yesterday evening it was all black and bare.
> And now it's covered with leaves.
> Estragon: Leaves?
> Vladimir: In a single night.
> Estragon: It must be the Spring.
> Vladimir: But in a single night! (42b)

---

[10] See "incongruities" and "style contrasts":
Booth 101.
[11] Shubert analyzes irony in nature:
Shubert 57.

The mysterious function of time is reflected in the protagonists' mindset and the boy's declarations about Godot's arrival. As the memory is based on time, the irregularities in the time progression question the verisimilitude of the memory. The protagonists' and boy's impossibility to remember the circumstances related to Godot's existence is similar in nature to Estragon's amnesia with respect to his boots. The protagonists are united in a realm of amnesia when they try to focus on their past experiences and surrounding circumstances. The concrete information is lost in the abyss of amnesia as if the stage shadows erased them. The spectator tentatively concludes that the repetition of events and the unexpected change in the tree's appearance point in the direction of a time game which remains beyond his comprehension.[12]

The amnesia of the boy's memory with respect to his previous encounter with the protagonists calls into question the chronology and reliability of his statements. The time plays with the protagonists just as they play with their hats and boots; the absence of a chronological sequence that would change the protagonists' situation makes the performance reiterative.

The performance of the play absorbs time and light, while the amnesia and darkness fill in the mental and dramatic space. The shadows and their prolongations invite the spectator to consider another reality of the stage which remains vague and shifting. The double visual representation of the characters, which is reflected in the shadows, corresponds to the lack of chronology in the play. Even though the shadows are disproportional to the size and shape of characters that they represent, they are more representative of the characters' existence than their testimonies that are inherently linked to time. The shadows remain connected to the

---

[12] Roster gives an example of the protagonist's incapacity to understand his destiny:

Roster 28-9.

physical form that shapes them, while the protagonists' narration is rife with fragmentation and inconsistencies.

The loss of memory is not adverse to the protagonists' expectations to see Godot. Without blotting out Godot's previous failures to appear, the protagonists' waiting game could be questioned. In order to preserve the structure of the play, its internal dynamics need to erase the indicators that question the existence of Godot and thus permit the play's scale to slightly tip toward a favorable outcome.

> I don't remember having met anyone yesterday. But to-morrow I won't remember having met anyone to-day. So don't count on me to enlighten you. (56b-57)

The protagonists perpetuate the game of memory cancellation in order to preserve the validity of their slogan: "Yes, in this confusion one thing alone is clear. We are waiting for Godot *to come*."[13] In the context of the representation, the certainty of Godot's arrival is an example of how the dramatic irony shores up the frail hope of seeing Godot. One can also dub this type of hope "feigned hope" as the protagonists manipulate the information in order to make the occurrence of an improbable event imminent.

The protagonists' verbal exchanges resemble a poem of the absurd in which the term "friends" is used as a rhyme. The dubious use of the word "friends" and Estragon's laughs indicate to the spectators that the characters never developed a friendship. Their amnesia cancels the possibility of a friendship that requires a continuum of a relationship that spans the gap between the past and the present. The concept of friendship acquires an additional dimension in the following passage:

---

[13]   Beckett. *Waiting for Godot*. 51. my italics.

Pozzo: I used to have a wonderful sight-but are you friends?
Estragon: (*laughing noisily*). He wants to know if we are friends!
Vladimir: No, he means friends of his. (54b.)

Pozzo's question about friendship remains ambiguous as neither the spectators nor the protagonists can deduce to whom the term "friends" refers. Is it a question of friendship between two groups: Pozzo and Lucky on one side and Vladimir and Estragon on the other? Or does Pozzo refer to the friendship between Vladimir and Estragon?

Pozzo's incapacity to recognize the voice of his "friends" reflects the situation of the protagonists who are unable to abandon the tree. Both cases are based on amnesia. Pozzo is unable to recognize the voices of his friends, while Estragon and Vladimir do not remember the reiterative announcements of Godot's arrival and his subsequent failure to appear. It is ironic that the amnesia has contradictory effects: it saves the protagonists from despair and sentences them to endless wait. As the cancellation of despair tends toward life and aimless waiting toward death, irony pulls the protagonists in opposite directions. These forces cancel themselves and the protagonists remain seated on their mound waiting for the solution.

Parallel Ironies

Since the second half of the twentieth century, *Waiting for Godot* has been performed around the globe and the concept of salvation has been the theme of numerous critical works. The purpose of this section of the book is to show how Vladimir and Estragon's efforts to change the stern conditions of the stage comply with the structure of irony. Ironic statements and situations shore up the protagonists' efforts to reach a state of well-being. The protagonists' behavior and statements remain coherent in the realms of reality and fantasy thanks to the unifying bond of irony.

The first contact between the protagonists and Pozzo reveals a series of characteristics that govern social relations on stage. Initially, Vladimir and Estragon wonder what they should do with Pozzo, who is pleading for help. Their subsequent interaction with him proves more dynamic and could be classified into three types of behavior: ignoring, abusing and helping. This enigmatic rapport is a reflection of the protagonists' mutual interaction. Vladimir and Estragon have ignored, threatened, abused and helped each other. Pozzo's appearance on the stage disrupts the bilateral relationship between the protagonists and forms a triangle. This new angle offers an opportunity to play old games in the newly formed group.

Spurred by enthusiasm, Vladimir and Estragon rush to Pozzo to experience new sensations. The protagonists manifest their personality with greater freedom in their interaction with Pozzo than with each other because he is defenseless. Pozzo's helpless posture, lying on the ground, and the absence of his friend Lucky make him vulnerable to Vladimir's and Estragon's impulses: "The best would be to take advantage of Pozzo's calling for help." (51)

The protagonists' cruelty is fundamental to the play's irony. As Vladimir and Estragon are already condemned to endless suffering in the form of a ceaseless wait, the spectator might expect them to focus their game on a more optimistic issue. But no, the protagonists heed the cries of desperation and seize the opportunity to immerse themselves in a game of suffering as if their own were not sufficient.[14] The scene in which the suffering couple delivers blows to another defenseless creature pro-

---

[14] In Happy Days, Winnie and Willie choose more pleasant themes to distract themselves.

jects an ironic panorama: sufferers promote suffering in the search for salvation.

The protagonists' observations and deductions regarding the infliction of punishment call to mind the proverbial concept of "two wrongs do not make a right". However, during the game of suffering that is focused on Pozzo, the protagonists seem to communicate, plan and collaborate better than when they are alone. As if their suffering were not sufficient, another's brings them together.

After a period of listening in total indifference to Pozzo's pleading for mercy[15], Vladimir suggests to Estragon that they give Pozzo a hand. Unexpectedly, the nature of the protagonists' game changes. The torturers offer a soothing hand to their victim: "Perhaps we could help him." (51b) This philanthropic suggestion is entwined with a mercantile stratagem: "We should ask him for a bone first. Then if he refuses we'll leave him there." (50b) In *Waiting for Godot*, the protagonists try to obtain things directly -by asking, searching or waiting- but in this case, Estragon takes advantage of the newly created situation to blackmail Pozzo. The audience winces at this scheme as it presents a twist in the protagonists' original behavior. Under the veil of the impulsive acting, the spectator sneaks a peek at the protagonists' plan to take advantage of Pozzo's situation. This sensation in the audience's mind makes the protagonists' performance more complex as their impulsiveness is coupled with premeditation.

In Pozzo's case, the protagonists physically abuse the defenseless newcomer; and in the case of their mutual interaction, the game is performed under the guise of verbal and mental wiles. In the latter case, the expressions of hope to see Godot and their plans to leave the "Godfor-

---

[15] For a better appreciation of the scenic effects, consult:
Emmanuel Jacquart. *Le Théâtre de dérision: Beckett, Ionesco, Adamov* (Paris: Gallimard, 1978)

saken turf" (42) form a verbal safety net[16]; while in the interaction with Pozzo, their intent to escape from reality takes on a physical guise. The two types of behavior form a paradigm in which the protagonists' and Pozzo's search for escape is based on verbal and physical manifestations.

Vladimir's question, "You mean we have him at our mercy?" (51b), marks the apex of the protagonists' supremacy on stage. Their erect posture with respect to Pozzo's prone position confirms that Vladimir and Estragon finally have somebody under their control. The exhilarating sensation of power is a marvelous catalyst in the dramatic performance of the play as the interaction with Pozzo offers an activity which is very distinct from the daily pretense of waiting for Godot. It gives the chance of a lifetime to be active, powerful and controlling. In this game, the protagonists make a dramatic reversal in their roles: instead of suffering, they make Pozzo suffer; instead of contemplating their own helplessness, they observe Pozzo's.[17] Hence, their interaction provides an ideal relief; their burden becomes another's.

During their sadistic manifestations, Vladimir and Estragon see Pozzo through a dehumanizing lens and try to define an adequate implementation of abuse: "Make sure he's alive before you start. No point in exerting yourself if he is dead." (56b) Pummeling an inanimate object should comply with the dubious function of a psychological catharsis but the protagonists need to "Make sure" that the victim is alive and consequently suffers. This sadistic requirement confounds the spectator and adds a wicked aspect to the protagonists' behavior that at times seemed to be based on purely mechanical reactions.

---

[16] Stanislavski elaborates the concept of "internal forces" which can be applied to Vladimir's and Estragon's relationship.

[17] See:

George Peterson. "Suffering in modern drama", *Literary Analysis* (Vol. 21. April 1992)

The confirmation that Pozzo is alive and the abuse that the protagonists wreak upon his defenseless body take an unexpected turn and the
paradigm "the suffering souls make another suffer" is replaced by its
opposite "the abused harms the abusers":

With sudden fury Estragon starts kicking Lucky, hurling abuse at him
as he does so. But he hurts his foot and moves away, limping and groa-
ning. (56b)

The dramatic reversal in the power balance is ironic as the power figure hurts himself in the act of abusing another. Pozzo was initially an
object of contemplation and abuse; and in the latter scene, he becomes a
player that influences the course of the game by hurting his foe. In the
new power distribution, the circle of interaction is completed with a
twist, the intention to hurt bounces back and hurts the villain.

In the midst of the chaotic games, the play gives a moral lesson to di-
sobedient children: one reaps what one sows.[18] The lesson is ironic since
the scenic context of the play seems void of all moral and ethical values.
The suffering of the protagonists is a gratuitous occurrence, and its cau-
sality remains beyond the spectators' scope of comprehension in the
realm of logic, time and space. However, the quaint lesson acquires new
dimensions as a sense of "justice" permeates the dramatic setting and
punishes Estragon. Characters initially perceived as victims, Vladimir
and Estragon, become objects of audience's derision as they intentionally
allot suffering to a helpless, blind man.

The noose of guilt tightens around Vladimir's and Estragon's game.
The audience "condemns" the protagonists to the well-deserved suffering
in which it discovered them when the curtains opened. The condemna-

---

[18] Nonetheless, the theater of the absurd and Samuel Beckett's drama are
considered amoral by the experts of Samuel Beckett's drama.

tion coincides with the protagonists' initial stage-imposed punishment that was the cause of the audience's commiseration. The difference between the two forms of punishment is that the protagonists' plight is the product of the play's setting from the opening of the curtains, while the audience's condemnation takes place during the unwinding of the play's plot.[19]

The puzzling aspect of the stage in which power, violence and futility entwine is intensified with the generous help that the protagonists offer to Pozzo. After thrashing him, the protagonists want to help:

Vladimir: He wants us to help him to get up.

Estragon: Then why don't we? What are we waiting for?

(*They help Pozzo to his feet, let him go. He falls.*)

Vladimir: We must hold him.

(*They get him up again. Pozzo sags between them, his arms round their necks.*) (54b)

Contradictory tendencies, abuse and help, represent the internal chaos in the protagonists' minds.[20]

The protagonists manifest the need to save Pozzo as they are unable to save themselves. The protagonists' projection on Pozzo reflects their identity crisis. Besides not knowing Pozzo, they do not know themselves. Vladimir and Estragon cannot understand their plight although they are steadfastly peering at its reflection in Pozzo. Seeing but not understanding is the enigma of the protagonists' situation.

---

[19]   In this case, the term "plot" refers merely to the sequence of events.

[20]   Bentley studies different types of impulses, sometimes contradictory, that the characters manifest on stage.

E. Bentley. *La vida del drama* (Mexico: Paidos Studio, 1982)

Godot's lack of identity contributes to Vladimir's and Estragon's confusion. It fluctuates from the concept of "savior" (32) to somebody who could harm them: "Your only hope left is to disappear. [. . .] *Estragon goes and crouches behind the tree.*" (47b-48) The margin of uncertainty indicates that the protagonists do not have the slightest idea about Godot's nature or disposition.

The incorporation of contradictory concepts into the play's structure, as we have seen in the tentative creation of Godot's identity, is also reflected in the ease with which the characters create and cancel diverse scenarios.[21] Both impulses, causing and resolving a dispute, stem from the sheer love for the game: "That's the idea, let's abuse each other. [. . .] Now let's make up." (48b). This type of inconsistency was also observed in their interaction with Pozzo. The oscillation between belligerent and pacific manifestations has no regulating mechanism. The protagonists immediately implemented into action words expressing intentions with respect to Pozzo.

The protagonists immediately abuse him or help him stand up. But when their intentions are self-centered, they dissipate as was the case with their plan to leave. The explanation for effective acting with respect to others and helplessness when focusing on themselves remains enigmatic.

The protagonists also consider the option of suicide. The purpose of the suicide is to provide an additional dimension to the search for a solution. From the protagonists' philosophical but foggy point of view, the inscrutable aspect of death is the key to an incomprehensible existence.[22]

---

[21]   Alain Robbe-Grillet explores the conjunction of stage and psychological elements in the creation of Beckett's dramatic space.

[22]   To see the dramatic effects created by the presence of death, consult:
Colin Duckworth. *Angels of Darkness: Dramatic Effect in Beckett and Ionesco* (London: George Allen & Unwin Ltd., 1972)

On the other hand, suicide is incongruent with the situation because the protagonists are resolving one unknown with another, life with death. The existential conundrum has an ironic dimension; trying to reconstruct their unstable existence, the protagonists risk pushing it over the rim of non-existence. At the impasse of existential doubts, Estragon suggests to Vladimir: "The best thing would be to kill me..." (40)

Suicide and definite departure remain on the level of conjecture because their carrying out would end the search for the solution to Vladimir's and Estragon's existence. The materialization of either of these two options, suicide or exit, would be incongruent with the nature of the play, which is based on endless searching.

The spectator starts perceiving the incompatible contradictions of staying and leaving, living and dying, as the basis for the play's performance. The general feeling of impossibility to change the situation spans the play, and the irony of hopeless search establishes a balance between opposite sides.

In the second phase of the play, the mental game is introduced as an escape stratagem. Vladimir tries to brainwash Estragon by infusing the concept of well-being into his mind: "You must be happy too, deep down, if you only knew it." (38b) In this statement, Vladimir's mental image represents the dramatic setting that the protagonists try to create on stage in order to continue playing the game of waiting. Vladimir tries to convince Estragon that he is happy and immune to suicide: "Say you are happy, even if it's not true." (39)

Vladimir's insistence on their state of well-being[23] proves to be fruitful and both enter into a frenetic reiteration of their declaration of happi-

---

[23] See the concept of happiness through "ironic creation" in Soren Kierkegaard's eminent work (the second part of the book):
Soren Kierkegaard. *The concept of Irony, With Constant Reference to Socrates* (Bloomington: Indiana University Press, 1968. Trans. Lee M. Capel).

ness: "I am happy", "So am I" (twice), "We are happy" (twice), etc. (39) The repetition of the statement "I am happy" is ironic as they are on the brink of suicide.[24] But their plight and the resulting need for a remedy catalyze their euphoric bursts of happiness. Although the exclamations of happiness seem to be a liberating element in the protagonists' plight, they are as ironic as the kicking of Pozzo. The illusion of well-being was construed with the intention of freeing the protagonists but it shackles them to the stage. The exclamations of happiness cancel their plans for escape by departure or suicide. This cancellation is based on the principle that since living conditions are good, there is no need to change. Consequently, exit or suicide are out of question. In this case, the irony is not based on the futility of the effort to escape but on the cancellation of the principal requirement for the change: the vile conditions under which they are living. Once reality is set aside, the play is immersed entirely into the domain of irony. The plot deviates from the search for the solution to the mental creation of an idyllic world.

The fluctuation in the characters' moods is not limited to the protagonists, it also involves Pozzo who was initially subjected to unfortunate experiments. Pozzo's involvement in wavering intentions, weak decisions and varying activities confirms the general mood of the stage in which instability is the only rule.

In Pozzo's perplexing soliloquy, the drastic changes in tone permit the spectator to perceive the incongruency between the imaginary and real worlds. The dramatic tone is based on the cumulative effect of gestures, voice inflections and the semantic content of the poetic inspiration:

---

[24] Kerbrat-Orecchioni elaborates the concept of antiphrasis in which the opposite poles of a personality or concept fuse together:
Kerbrat-Orecchioni 195-221.

[...] (*lyrical*) tirelessly torrents of red and white light it begins to lose its effulgence, to grow pale [. . .] pale, ever a little paler, a little paler until (*dramatic pause* [. . .]) pppfff!!! finished! *It comes to rest.*[25] But- (*hand raised in admonition*)-but behind this veil of gentleness and peace night is charging (*vibrantly*) and will burst upon us (*snaps his fingers*) pop! like that! (25b)

The dramatic intensification in Pozzo's inspiration, punctuated by lyricism and the profusion of colorful lights, spurs the creation of delusions. The flux of inspiration is intensified by pauses and vocal inflections as the playwright points out in the stage directions: "dramatic pause" and "vibrantly". These changes indicate the creation of a setting distinct from the circumstances in which the protagonists live, similar to the scene of the euphoric exclamations "we are happy!" (39) Nonetheless, Pozzo's warning gesture[26] uncovers the burden hidden under the ironic guise of a charming evening and, effectively, an instant later, the light and inspiration fade away.

Pozzo's poetic and dramatic performance with respect to the "charming night" and its "veil of gentleness and peace" (25b) force the spectator to interpret the idyllic descriptions warily. The lyricism subtly reveals the protagonists' tragedy[27] and uncovers a nightmare which does not vanish despite the poetic creativity. The ending of Estragon's lyrical inspiration, tainted with a nuance of vulgarity, confirms the protagonists' incapacity to cancel the scenic conditions and to preserve the ambiance of an enchanting evening.

---

[25]　My emphasis.

[26]　Beckett himself refers to the raising of the hand as "admonition". Beckett 25b.

[27]　Simon Benett explores different types of drama in: Simon Benett. *Tragic drama and the family: Psychoanalytic studies from Aeschylus to Beckett* (Yale University Press: New Haven, 1988) 274.

(*his inspiration leaves him*) just when we least expect it. (*Silence. Gloomily.*) That's how it is on this bitch of an earth. (25b)

The dreadful reality neutralizes the efforts of Pozzo's dramatic and poetic creativity. Just as Pozzo snaps his fingers, the enchanting evening vanishes and unveils the protagonists' reality. The inspiration remains a testimony to the ironic poetry which intended to transform the waning light into a luminous effervescence.

During the performance of the last two passages cited above, the spectator feels the change in the linguistic and dramatic tone.[28] Pozzo's attempt to create a new world through his poetic inspiration represents the dire need to transform his existence into a game of hypothetical possibilities. The ironic veil and its illusionary effect fade away with the pale scenic lights and force the protagonists to readapt themselves to their previous condition. The return to a passive tone and slow enunciation at the end of the poetic presentation indicate the end of one dramatic inspiration and the beginning of the next.

Once the poetic game ends and its lyrical effects dissipate, the protagonists go back to their wavering hope which borders on suicide. The protagonists compensate anew for their incapacity to change the situation with the playful explanation that their situation is not negative: "One knows what to expect." (25b.) Pozzo confirms this hypothesis about their well-being, "No further need to worry", and the game of ironic creations takes the form of a complacent custom: "We're used to it." (25b)

The return to the customary situation, "we are used to it", is a partial admittance that the cancellation of reality, either by Vladimir's and Estragon's euphoric proclamation of happiness or by Pozzo's lyrical profu-

---

[28] See:

    Betty Rojtman. *Forme et Signification dans le Théâtre de Beckett* (Paris: Nizet, 1976)

sion, has been stemmed by an unavoidable return to the on-stage reality. The opposite aspects of these attempts, one highly terse and reiterative and the other lyrical and ever-changing, underline the play's very nature: the search for salvation changes without dying out.

The ironic games that took place during the dramatic representation of physical violence, philanthropic help and the creation of the imaginary world involve the protagonists and spectators in a search for a solution to the protagonists' plight. The search is not conclusive but the protagonists' and spectators' exploring paths intertwine in an inextricable bond of mutual dependency that perpetuates the search for salvation.

Bibliography

Beckett, Samuel. *Waiting for Godot*. New York: Grove Press, 1972.

Beckett, Samuel. *Happy Days*. New York: Grove Press, 1961.

Álvarez, A. *Samuel Beckett*. New York: The Viking Press, 1973.

Anders, Günther. "Being without time: On Beckett's Play 'Waiting for Godot'". *Samuel Beckett, A collection of critical essays.* Ed. Martin Esslin. New Jersey: Prentice Hall, 1965.

Benett, Simon. *Tragic drama and the family: Psychoanalytic studies from Aeschylus to Beckett.* Yale University Press: New Haven, 1988.

Bentley, E. *La vida del drama*. Mexico: Paidos Studio, 1982.

Booth, Wayne C. *A Rhetoric of Irony.* Chicago: University of Chicago Press, 1974.

Duckworth, Colin. *Angels of Darkness: Dramatic Effect in Beckett and Ionesco.* London: George Allen & Unwin Ltd., 1972.

Kerbrat-Orecchioni, Catherine. "La ironía como tropo". *De la Ironía a lo grotesco.* Ed. Hernán Silva. Mexico: Universidad Metropolitana Iztapalapa, 1992. 195-221. Trans. Pilar Hernández Cobos.

Kierkegaard, Soren. *The concept of Irony, With Constant Reference to Socrates.* Bloomington: Indiana University Press, 1968. Trans. Lee M. Capel.

Peterson, George. "Suffering in modern drama". *Literary Analysis,* Vol. 21. April 1992.

Robbe-Grillet, Allain. "Samuel Beckett, or 'Presence' in the Theater". *Samuel Beckett, A collection of critical essays.* Ed. Martin Esslin. New Jersey: Prentice Hall, 1965.

Roster, Peter J. *La ironía como método de análisis literario: la poesía de Salvador Novo.* Madrid: Gredos, 1978.

Rojtman, Betty. *Forme et Signification dans le Théâtre de Beckett.* Paris: Nizet, 1976.

Stanislavski, Constantin. *Un actor se prepara.* Mexico: Editorial Diana, 1994.

Toro, Fernando de. "El discurso teatral". *Semiótica del teatro.* Carleton: Editorial Galerna, 1994.

Wellershoff, Dieter. "Failure of an Attempt at De-Mythologization: Samuel Beckett's Novels". *Samuel Beckett, A collection of critical essays.* Ed. Martin Esslin. New Jersey: Prentice Hall, 1965.

Wright, Edward. *Para comprender el teatro actual.* Mexico: Fondo de Cultura Económica, 1978.

Irony of Separation, *Endgame*

Structural and dramatic ironies represent the pillars of *Endgame*. The structural irony is based on a possible change in the play's unfolding, while the dramatic irony focuses on the preservation of the play's *status quo*.

The structural irony in *Endgame* reflects Kierkegaard's theory according to which the ironic hero, in this case Clov, cancels the real world in order to create his subjective reality. In the process of cancellation of the old and the creation of the new world, the ironist tries to liberate himself from the repressive limitations of reality in order to move to a superior level of existence. In Clov's case, this feat translates into leaving permanently the stage and its denizen Hamm.

The concepts of "general" and "dramatic irony" that were elaborated by Hutcheon, Booth, Glicksberg and other critics contribute to the clarification of the dramatic irony in *Endgame*. The complementary perspectives of these critics will be focused on forces that prevent Clov from leaving.[1] In this essay, the dramatic irony branches in two directions,

---

[1] Ironic and general ironies can be studied in:

toward the spectator and the protagonists. It emerges from the implicit messages that flow from the stage toward the audience and suggests that Clov's exit is highly improbable, reflecting Vellacott and Roster's dramatic irony.[2]

The two extensions of dramatic irony -one directed toward the spectator and the other toward the protagonists- often overlap in order to complement each other and counteract the structural irony that consists of Clov's negation and mental reconstruction of reality. Both aspects of dramatic irony, one focused on convincing the spectator that Clov's exit is impossible and the other on the cancellation of Clov's exit, hobble the protagonist's liberation.[3] The two ironies and their contrary functions alternate in the dramatic process of liberation and retention of Clov.

Linda Hutcheon. "Ironía, sátira, parodia. Una aproximación pragmática a la ironía". *De la Ironía a lo grotesco*. Ed. Hernán Silva. Trans. Pilar Hernández Cobos (Mexico: Universidad Metropolitana Iztapalapa, 1992) 173-4.

Wayne C. Booth, *A Rhetoric of Irony* (Chicago: University of Chicago Press, 1974) 102.

Charles Irving Glicksberg. *The ironic vision in modern literature* (The Hugue: Martinus Nijhoff) 44.

Northrop Frye. *Anatomy of Criticism, Four Essays* (New York: Atheneum, 1968) 63-5.

[2] Vellacott and Roster define dramatic irony as the spectator's knowledge about the protagonists' destiny that they ignore:

Philip Vellacott. *Ironic drama* (London: Cambridge University Press, 1975) 23-4.

Peter J. Roster. *La ironía como método de análisis literario: la poesía de Salvador Novo* (Madrid: Gredos, 1978) 14.

[3] Kenner elaborates the notion of a closed universe that hobbles the protagonist:

Hugh Kenner. "Shades of Syntax". *Samuel Beckett: a collection of criticism*. Ed. Ruby Cohn (New York: McGraw-Hill Book Company, 1975) 45.

Structural Irony

Clov initiates the elaboration of the structural irony following Kierkegaard's steps.[4] In the first phase, the protagonist tries to cancel the stage setting and, in the second, wander into new territories. The incipient cancellation of reality manifests itself in Clov's intention to leave. The highly-placed windows seem to be beyond Clov's reach and his nervous stride to and fro reflects his wish to project himself outward. The size of the windows and the protagonist's vain efforts to reach them place him in the problematic situation of striving against odds to peep at new horizons.

Once the spectator feels Clov's intention to leave, he senses that the resolving of the stage puzzle will require the understanding of the principles of cancellation of reality and the protagonist's intention to adopt new roles that will permit him to escape.

The relations that are established between the protagonists have an adverse effect on Clov's departure.[5] He tries to cancel their bond using the terms "mean" and "something" that Hamm has used previously to galvanize their relationship.

---

[4] Soren Kierkegaard. *The concept of Irony, With Constant Reference to Socrates.* Trans. Lee M. Capel (Bloomington: Indiana University Press, 1968) 265-289.

[5] On various occasions, Hamm reminds Clov that he is his father and that he saved his life.

Beckett. *Endgame.* 38.

In addition, Hamm plays a role that complies with paternal characteristics. For a better idea about filial relations in *Endgame*, I recommend:

Stanley Gontarski, *The Theatrical Notebooks of Samuel Beckett. Endgame* (Grove Press and Faber and Faber, 1993)

Stanley Gontarski, *The Intent of Undoing in Samuel Beckett's Dramatic Texts* (Indiana UP, 1985)

Hamm: We're not beginning to... to... mean something?
Clov: Mean something! You and I, mean something!
(*Brief laugh.*)
Ah that's a good one! (32)

Clov deconstructs the term "we" dividing it into its complementary parts: "you" and "I". This stratagem has the purpose of counteracting Hamm's intention to place the protagonists in the same social nucleus "we". In his effort to disrupt the order of things, Clov uses derision to demean the expression "mean something". Clov's brief laugh accompanies his statements and intensifies the negation of Hamm's message, while pointing toward the rupture of their union.[6] The laugh's disdainful aspect represents the play's structure under whose weight the stage cracks and a new reality emerges.

The spectator senses the importance of social unity, "we", and its potential value on the spiritual level: "mean something". Hamm's behavior confirms the spectator's interpretation as he insists on their union despite Clov's mockery. Hamm's insistence reinforces dramatic irony and counteracts Clov's disdainful perspective:

And without going so far as that, we ourselves... (*with emotion*)... we ourselves... at certain moments... (*Vehemently.*) To think perhaps it won't have been for nothing! (33)

The affective bond that Hamm extends toward his companion is a weapon in the fray for the possession of Clov and the cancellation of structural irony. The absence of Hamm's gestures and movements intensifies the dramatic effect of his verbal message.

---

[6] Hutcheon elaborates the concept of opposite meanings: Hutcheon 173.

As Clov does not manage to cancel definitely statements like "we ourselves", he is forced to seek a new tool. His newly-forged method consists of changing the direction of the conversation without any consideration for the previous statements. The fragmentation of the conversation undermines Hamm's effort to retain Clov.[7] For the implementation of interruption, Clov chooses the nature of the flea as the object and method of conversation. Skipping from one theme to another, like a flea from one spot to another, Clov initiates a conversation whose purpose is to negate and not to communicate. The focus on the flea complies with Clov's urgent need to change the direction of Hamm's statements about their relation and sidetrack it.

Clov needs to unburden himself of the moral and ethical weight, that presses upon him and keeps him by his paralyzed "father"[8], in order for the negation[9] of reality to occur. In fact, Clov is at the crossroads of a double cancellation: he needs to negate his filial responsibility and abandon his father. He accomplishes the first step by distancing himself from his father. He initiates the separation questioning the responsibility of his father in his past decisions. As Hamm left Mother Pegg to die in the darkness, Clov might be allowed to reiterate his father's deeds:

When old Mother Pegg asked you for oil for her lamp and you told her to get out to hell, you knew what was happening then, no? (*Pause.*) You know what she died of, Mother Pegg? Of darkness. (75)

---

[7] The fact that a paralyzed person tries to immobilize, metaphorically speaking, somebody who has no physical limitations represents an internal irony.

[8] See: footnote 5.

[9] I use the term "negation" in the Kierkegaardian sense of the word: cancellation.

After all, one condemnation to death by abandonment is justified by another. The sentencing to death by "darkness" loses its grisly aspect and gets catalogued as a family custom.

The moral justification that Clov elaborates using the abandonment of Mother Pegg and the location of his grandparents, Nagg and Nell, in the trash cans unites and separates the protagonists. It places Hamm and Clov into the same family unit and at the same time tears them apart under the guise of family morality. In other words, they are destined to remain in the same family; and at the same time, the abandonment sets them apart. The unifying and separating aspect of this scene is representative of the opposite forces that the dramatic and structural ironies represent.

Clov questions the logic of his confinement: "Why this farce, day after day?" (32) in an effort to cancel dramatic reality. As a convincing response remains beyond his reach, Clov deduces that the only reason for the perpetuation of his situation is the routine, just as Hamm confirms it: "Routine." (32) The trivial aspect of their interaction allows Clov to suggest that their relationship can be ended at any time. As there is no practical reason for the family ties to be preserved, Clov makes the second step in the structural irony: the creation of the subjective reality as a way of liberation à la Kierkegaard.

The change from blind obedience to the tentative projection outward is metaphorically represented in the scene with the telescope. Clov steps aside from Hamm ignoring his orders, "Don't leave me there!" (76), and takes the telescope. He climbs a ladder and once at the window level directs his telescope outward. The resolute aspect of Clov's posture is distinct from his hesitant steps and vain attempts to reach the windows at the opening scene. Clov has torn himself apart from the past and created an illusion of time progression; the dramatic present is distinct from the past and thus lays the foundation of the structural irony. His vague intention to separate himself from Hamm, which the spectator felt in the beginning of the play, is manifested by his visual projection outward. The multiple interpretations of the surrounding, which vary from the view of the ocean to the desert, temporarily free Clov through the creation of the subjective world.

In the telescope scene, the creation of the new reality is sought in two different manners: the protagonist's visual projection and his imagination. These methods of projection permit Clov to crack the vicious confinement of routine.

> Clov: (*He gets down, picks up the telescope, turns it on auditorium.*)
> I see... a multitude... in transports... of joy.
> (*Pause.*)
> That's what I call a magnifier.
> (*He lowers the telescope, turns towards Hamm.*)
> Well? Don't we laugh? (29)

The comment about the exuberant joy of the spectators is exaggerated, it even brings to mind the form of a farce, but the purpose of Clov's poetic creation is precisely the elaboration of a setting that is diametrically opposed to the one in which he lives.[10]

The spectator feels a shiver as he listens to Clov. The contrast between the spectator's state of mind and the description, "a multitude in transports of joy" (29), is analogous to Clov's situation and the ambiance

---

[10] Godin and Kenner elaborate a concept that complements Kierkegaard's view about the "problematic verisimilitude" of the facts:

Georges Godin and Michaël La Chance. *Beckett, Entre le refus de l'art et le parcours mystique* (Canada: Le Castor Astral, 1994) 43 and 48.

Hugh Kenner. «Samuel Beckett: Comedian of the Impasse.» *The Stoic Comedians, Flaubert, Joyce, and Beckett* (Berkeley, Los Angeles, London: University of California Press, 1974) 67-8.

that he seeks when he projects his gaze toward the audience. The inter-pretation of the spectator's feelings, "a multitude in transports of joy", is a reflection of the protagonist's wishes and at the same time the starting point in the decoding of the play by the spectator. The spectator realizes that the deformation of reality is the goal of Clov's imagination and he takes on the task of decoding Clov's intention.

The telescope's capacity to change the geographic characteristics is combined with the possibility to alter the spectators' state of mind. The telescope represents the instrument of poetic creation thanks to which the protagonist discovers new aspects in life and communicates them to the audience. The telescope also permits Clov to transfer his imaginary im-pression of joy from his psyche to the auditorium. The joy that at times reaches the dimensions of an enrapture is the seed of structural irony that Clov plants on the sterile soil of the stage in order to topple the general order of the play.

The crystallization of Clov's intention to free himself manifests itself in the announcement of his departure.[11] In order to implement this step, Clov prepares himself and Hamm for the separation. On the one hand, the separation is based on the interruption of Clov's customary presence by Hamm's side: "Soon I won't do it any more." (43) On the other, Clov announces his exit: "I'll leave you." (39) Both statements serve as the foreshadowing of a definite separation of the protagonists and represent respectively the steps that lead to liberation according to Kierkegaard's theory: first, the negation and then, liberation. The negation of the first step is also reflected in the use of the negative form: "I won't do it..."

During the planning of the exit, Clov seems to be without a clue about the world that surrounds him. The visual images that the telescope

---

[11] Pavis concentrates on "action" during the representation:
Patrice Pavis. "Performance analysis: Space, Time, Action". *Gestos, Teo-ría y práctica del teatro hispánico* (Year 11. N. 22. November 1996) 11.

provides are incongruent because of their incompatibility. The reiteration of Clov's intention to leave suggests the protagonist's hesitation to undertake the trip. Even though he does not have any reliable information about the outside world, his plan to leave is substantiated by the deterioration of his situation on stage. The announcements of Clov's departure, "I'll leave you" (58), are mixed with a threatening notion of the unknown that undermines his plan of evasion. The reiteration of the intention to leave undermines itself and thus questions the feasibility of the structural irony.

Approaching the end of the representation, Clov verbalizes his mental image in which he leaves his room and takes the path of happiness: "I open the door of the cell and go. [...] When I fall I'll weep for happiness." (81) The spectator has to ask himself if these words reflect a blueprint of Clov's plan or a projection of his wish. Both options find their dramatic justification in the unfolding of the play. The intention to leave is announced with more resolve in the last stretch of the representation, albeit Clov's mind might be compensating its incapacity to act with fantasy. The two possibilities fit in Kierkegaard's theoretical framework: liberation through the creation of the imaginary world and the adoption of a new lifestyle to fit the novel context.

Clov's intentions to put in order the things on the stage reflect a need to minimize his confusion. The scenic austerity that characterizes Beckett's plays contributes an ironic sense to Clov's efforts to put his belongings in order.

> Clov: Putting things in order.
> (*He straightens up. Fervently.*)
>> I'm going to clear everything away!
>> (*He starts picking up again.*)
>> [...] I love order it's my dream. (57)

Underneath the comical aspect of Clov's words lies the protagonist's effort to free himself. The spectator observes how the mental state of the protagonist grapples with his inexorable situation. The deterioration of Clov's sight, increased pain in his legs and the realization that his thinking capacity is decreasing show to the spectator that the protagonist's life is waning. In this plight, Clov establishes a bond with the spectator as they both try and fail to find a way to invert the process of deterioration.[12]

Hamm manifests symptoms of confusion similar to Clov's. He is unable to put in order the things that surround him because he is blind and paralyzed, but he tries to resolve his problematic situation with the use of dramatic space. Hamm's demand to be placed in the center of the room seems to provide him with special gratification. Besides a possible feeling of authority and power, Hamm's place in the center of the room serves as a point of reference for Clov that should move around him. The central position of Hamm serves as the counterweight for Clov's intention to leave and thus a pillar of dramatic irony that prevents the crumbling of the protagonist's confinement. The structural irony that Clov tries to incorporate into the dramatic space is meant to lean heavily against the pillar that Hamm erects in the middle of the stage.

When the two sides seem to drift apart, they unexpectedly reach a consensus in order to realize a triumphant exit. Hamm suggests to Clov:

> Let's go from here, the two of us! South! You can make a raft and the currents will carry us away, far away, far away, to other... mammals!"
> (34)

---

[12] Beckett. Endgame. 46.

This suggestion is unique in the unfolding of the play as it proposes an explicit plan for the escape from the stage and at the same time involves both protagonists. Curiously enough both ironies are included in this scheme. On the one hand, dramatic irony is preserved as Clov remains by Hamm's side; and on the other, structural irony is at least partially implemented as Clov disrupts his ties with the stage and leaves.

Thanks to Hamm's proposition, a glimmer of hope sparks on stage. The representation might drastically veer and the stage could be transformed like the tree in *Waiting for Godot*. Clov's acceptance of Hamm's proposal supports this expectation and for the first time the exit plan is supported by both protagonists.

This agreement is more credible than Clov's reiterative threats: "I'll leave you." (12) Leaving together makes the separation from their residence easier to perform because it avoids the difficulties that the separation of the protagonists implies. In addition to their unity, the protagonists' tentative agreement presents a simple and logical procedure that increases the possibility of their success: the creation of the raft with a sail and the use of the currents. Their logical plan and agreement give a sense of probability to their rafting trip into the unknown.

The lack of adequate conditions, such as the presence of a large body of water, places in doubt the plan to use a raft and sail away. The stage-imposed limitations reinforce the dramatic irony and sink the plan of the navigational enterprise. The absence of water and the imaginary sharks drain surreptitiously the reservoir of Clov's possibilities and steer the spectator's expectations in the direction of dramatic irony.

Dramatic Irony

In Clov's and Hamm's interaction, the former seeks the cancellation of their coexistence, while the latter tries to preserve it. Clov's evasion hinges on the cancellation of their social ties and Hamm's efforts to preserve them. In this situation of adversity, the introduction of a furtive rat permits the elaboration of the structural irony by Clov and triggers Hamm's retort that reinforces dramatic irony:

> Clov: He [the rat]'s got away.
> Hamm: He can't go far.
> (*Pause. Anxious.*)
> Eh?
> Clov: He doesn't need to go far. (71)

Clov uses the rat's flight to allude to his wish of evasion. Hamm responds to the threat by predicting the rat's failure to get away.

The threat is a tool in Clov's and Hamm's schemes. The former implemented it metaphorically into the elaboration of his exit and the latter into the cancellation of Clov's escape "He can't go far." In both cases, the threat has the function of hobbling the opponent's intentions.

The rat represents a concrete manifestation of Clov's escape. It is no longer a gaze that is projected outward but a representation of a physical transition from one world into another that carries along Clov's hopes. Clov's escape would imply the death of the blind and paralyzed protagonist, while Clov's staying would further his mental and physical deterioration. It is possible that the protagonists do not realize the dangers of the ironic game that they play but the accomplishment of either wish would cause the automatic cancellation of the other.[13]

The implementation of dramatic irony is based on a double negation. First, Hamm cancels the rat by suspending him in the unfathomable darkness. Second, Hamm's blindness and paralysis obstruct Clov's exit. In other words, Hamm projects his negativism and weakness upon the image of Clov's salvation in order to transform it into nothingness.

Objects play an important role in Hamm's implementation of dramatic irony. When he orders Clov to bring a biscuit for Nagg, he revives family ties. The biscuit establishes a triangular relationship between three generations: son, father and grandfather.[14] The father who orders his son to help his grandfather recreates an image of a family:

Hamm: Give him [Nagg] a biscuit.
(*Exit Clov.*) ...
(*Enter Clov with biscuit.*)
Clov: I'm back with the biscuit.
(*He gives biscuit to Nagg who fingers it, sniffs it.*) (10)

The biscuit doubles the presence of handicapped people on stage. The spectator was aware of Hamm's incapacity to walk from the very opening of the curtains but the biscuit brings forth another family member, Nagg, that can not or at least appears not to be able to move about. At this point of the dramatic representation, Hamm's position in the center of the room loses its strategic function and the dramatic focus is placed on Clov. His location at the midpoint of an imaginary line that

---

[13] About the knowledge and understanding of the spectator, see:
Vellacott 23-4.
Roster 14.
[14] Beckett. *Endgame.* 38 and 48-9.

bridges the gap between his father and grandfather forces him to adopt the role of a provider. Nagg's desperate cries for his "pap" (9-10) reinforce Hamm's array of demands that shackle Clov to his side.

The spectator, and maybe Clov himself, does not know whether Nagg is capable of eating the biscuit. The sniffing and fingering of the biscuit by Nagg contradict the desperate pleadings for it and call into question its consumption. Nonetheless, the biscuit's function remains anchored in the dramatic irony that allows the elders to tighten their grip on Clov. The activity related to the providing of the biscuit plunges Clov into an activity that reinforces his obligation to help family members.

The biscuit represents the countermeasure to Hamm's actions related to Mother Pegg. It becomes the extension of dramatic irony through a revival of responsibilities that shackle Clov to the imaginary line that runs from Hamm to Nagg. As Clov invents a rat to help him escape from the stage, Hamm provides a biscuit that ends up in Nagg's hands just as Clov ends up anew in Hamm's clutches.

Hamm's collocation in the center of the room and the use of the biscuit are esthetically related to the circle and functionally to a rotational movement. The spectator is tempted to place these circular forms in a context of futile games.[15] Nonetheless, if the spectator adopts a cosmic perspective of the situation and remains in the realm of ludic creation, he might observe Hamm's metamorphosis in a Kafkian manner. Hamm becomes a planet around which Clov rotates incessantly; and thus, the circular movement becomes a function of the dramatic irony.

Automatic obedience represents a major pillar in Hamm's dramatic irony. He systematically and without any apparent need proceeds with a

---

[15] The lack of logic has a comical aspect in:
   Maurice Nadeau. "Samuel Beckett: Humor and the Void". *Samuel Beckett, A collection of critical essays*. Ed. Martin Esslin (New Jersey: Prentice Hall, 1965) 33.

litany of orders that Clov executes without any reckoning. The spectator has repeatedly witnessed Clov's humble obedience when Hamm insisted on being moved to and fro in search of the exact center of the room. The situation is ironic as the physically more active and independent person, Clov, remains hobbled by his inverted image, Hamm. Once more, the spectator observes a cosmic representation in which a satellite orbits around a stationary planet.

Hamm's language does not always take an imperative tone as was seen in the scene about the search of the center of the room. At times, his voice becomes tender and pleading for attention even though his language remains direct:

Hamm: It's time for my story. Do you want to listen to my story?
Clov: No.
Hamm: Ask my father if he wants to listen to my story. (48)

Clov's laconic response, "No", reflects his resistance to Hamm's dramatic irony, but Hamm insists on the narration of his story in order to reinforce the social bond that unites them. Finally, Hamm manages to convince his father to listen to him and as Clov remains in the room, he also becomes a receptor. Clov's initial refusal to listen becomes an acceptance because his physical presence on stage and his propensity to listen overshadow his negative response.

Hamm's narration also projects the inverse image of the story that Clov told about his father's abandonment of Mother Pegg. Instead of a person who leaves a family member to die, Hamm depicts himself as somebody who helps an unknown child to survive:

"In the end he asked me would I consent to take in the child as well-if he were still alive." (53)

The two contrasting stories represent the complementary parts of a standoff in which the views, words and actions clash and perpetuate the fray between the dramatic and structural ironies.

It is possible that the narration of the story has the purpose of alluding to Hamm's adoption of Clov. And if Clov identifies himself as the child who was saved by Hamm, the structural irony will be brought to a stalemate and Clov's responsibility to help Hamm will be transformed into an obligation.

In the context of Clov's childhood, the biscuit has the purpose of recreating an image in Clov's mind in which Hamm plays the paternal role of a provider. If this hypothesis is true, Clov might have been introduced into an activity that has been performed during his childhood by Hamm. Seen under this light, Hamm's burden and obligation are inherited by Clov.

The fragmented nature of the protagonists' conversations and the scarce information about the stage setting prevent the spectator or the reader of the play from making definite conclusions about Hamm's intentions or the characters' past. The inconclusiveness of this hypothesis maintains the spectator and the reader in a state of dubious contemplation.

Under the guise of a conversation and with the offer of a biscuit to his moribund father, Hamm seeks an appropriate conduit to Clov's affective side. He manages to mask his intentions to create social ties with Clov thanks to a veil of disinterested comments and futile tasks.[16]

The concept of time plays an important role in Hamm's intent to bring Clov to a standstill. It is introduced into the play through the botanical facet of their conversation. Hamm broaches the issue of time

---

[16] The stage contributes to the unfolding of the plot:

Denis Diderot. *La Paradoja del comediante* (Mexico: Colección Temas Teatrales, 1979) 64.

pointing out that the seeds that Clov has planted never sprouted in order to implement the concept of immutability or immobility. Hamm's subterfuge becomes fruitful as Clov lets out a stream of comments about seeds' infertility: "They haven't sprouted.", "If they were going to sprout they would have sprouted." and "They'll never sprout!" (13)

Clov's negative attitude with respect to the sprouting of the seeds reflects Hamm's "good job" in stifling Clov's hope to witness a new form of life or adopt new ideas on stage. As if Hamm wanted to make a concluding remark about their *modus vivendi*, he states: "It's the end of the day like any other day, isn't it, Clov?" (13) His statement is a blend of an affirmative and interrogative form as if it were representing the nature of the whole play in which a concept overlaps its opposite: certainty and doubt or affirmation and negation. In the combination of opposite forms and expressions, the impossibility to change the protagonists' situation persists.

Besides time, Hamm manipulates Clov's concept of space. He creates spatial limits in Clov's mind that coincide with the parameters of the stage. As a consequence of this mental blueprint, Clov's movement is limited to stage planks.

In a moment of rebellious enthusiasm, Clov informs Hamm that he is leaving. Hamm immediately anticipates the whereabouts of Clov's movement: "In the kitchen?" (12) As Clov confirms his final destination, "the kitchen", Hamm continues to investigate and define Clov's further activities. The volley of Hamm's questions and suggestions, *a priori* naive, stymies Clov's movement and thinking process. Hamm intertwines his questions with Clov's answers to create an impression of a collaborative plan that is based on routine activities firmly anchored to the stage.

Even though Hamm persuades Clov that the physical limits of the stage enclose the entire space that is available to them, he contradicts himself by describing the world beyond. Thus, the inner world becomes even more restrained as the outside exerts an inward pressure on it thanks to its primary components: death and darkness.[17] The discussion about Mother Pegg and the rat contribute to the general tone of the representation: "Infinite emptiness will be all around you all the resurrected dead of all the ages wouldn't fill in..." (36)

Besides the manipulation of the concepts of time and space, Hamm grafts new feelings into Clov's psyche: "My house a home for you." (38) This laconic comment reinforces dramatic irony on the affective level and creates the concept of home as a refuge in which Hamm offers a safe haven to Clov. Under the guise of hospitality, Hamm disorients Clov and transforms their collective nightmare into a notion of well-being. The ironic use of the term "home" erases Clov's personal experiences and engraves Hamm's message of hospitality. If Hamm manages to realize this rotation of concepts, Clov will remain in his *home*. The rotation of concepts, "prison" vs. "home", is a mental game that reflects Vladimir's and Estragon's game with hats in *Waiting for Godot*. One concept is replaced by another; in the first case the mechanism is founded on the abstract image of "home", and in the second, on hats.

Manipulating the parameters of reality, time and space, Hamm creates a concept of home in Clov's mind that bears resemblance to Nagg's and Nell's trash cans. In Clov's case, Hamm personally plants the seeds of metaphorical images that sprout in his son's mind; while in the communication with his parents, Hamm uses Clov to implement his orders: "Bottle [Nagg]!" (10) In either case, Hamm's hobbling stunt is skillfully

---

[17] Worth studies space and its role in drama:
    Katherine Worth. "The space and the sound in Beckett's theater". *Beckett the shape changer*. Ed. Katherine Worth (London: Routledge & Kegan Paul, 1975) 183.

applied and Clov, Nagg and Nell remain entangled in the dramatic net of their boss.

Even though the claustrophobic space of the trash cans implies a condemnation to darkness, as was the rat's destiny, Nagg and Nell find a refuge in it. The elders' feeling of security in their residences is suggested by their behavior. They lift the trash can lids, plead for food, complain about their physical deterioration and fantasize about love scenes, but they never ask to be taken out or try to get out of the trash cans. Their space is delimited by the round, metallic walls inside of which they pass their time. Both the darkness and the rat's limited runaway are embodied in Nagg's and Nell's situation. The couple is sentenced to life in darkness and they certainly can not go far unless their trash cans get rolled away. Even if this occurs, they will remain in the same space and darkness as the rat.

In Hamm's dramatic irony, the principle of enclosing and immobilizing is reflexive. The order that Hamm directs to Clov regarding the bottling of Nagg is executed promptly, but by obeying Hamm's demand, Clov bottles himself also because Nagg represents the family tradition. The imprisoning effect of this scene is transitive and reflexive. The idea sprouts in Hamm's mind, moves to Clov, from Clov to Nagg, and bounces back to Clov. The caroming effect of the dramatic irony manifests its capacity to change its nature, an idea turns into a word and the word into a mental state. This process of transformation was also observed in the case of the rat that became a threat and it subsequently reflects Clov's mental state.

The similarity between Clov and the elders is also apparent in their physical deterioration. The elders' difficulty in consuming the biscuit is reflected in Clov's gradual loss of sight and mobility.[18] On the linguistic

---

[18] Beckett. *Endgame.* 35.

and existential levels, Clov's statement of confusion is echoed by Nagg as they both ask: "Why this farce, day after day?" (14, 32) Their age difference brings back the notion of time. The spectator observes two stages of the same person as their common existential doubts bring them together.

Hamm's whistle plays a significant role in the protagonists' communication. Its first echoes communicate a dire need for attention but the despotic voice that follows transforms them into orders. Clov's rushes to the wheelchair indicate that the whistle exercises an irrevocable power to summon him. As the whistle does not belong to the realm of language, it does not give an opportunity to Clov to argue or contradict its message.

The direction of the whistle's message is unilateral. It is transmitted by Hamm and directed toward Clov and the spectator. Nonetheless, as in the case of bottling, Clov attributes to the whistle a reflexive property as he rushes to Hamm's side. In a certain manner, the sound bounces back to the sender. The whistle's function is to check once more Clov's exit and bring him to the center. The way Clov bottles himself by enclosing Nagg in the trash can, Hamm shuts himself in the dramatic space by bringing Clov to his side. The whistle's eloquence has promoted Hamm's dramatic irony by anchoring both protagonists to the stage and isolating them from the *outside darkness*.

The affective side of the notions that Hamm uses complements the demanding echoes of the whistle:

Hamm: If you leave me how shall I know?
Clov (*briskly*): Well you simply whistle me and if I don't come running it means I've left you.
(*Pause.*)
Hamm: You won't come and kiss me goodbye? (45)

The hypothetical ignoring of the whistle forebodes Clov's exit. It is not a well-defined announcement of departure but an insinuation to it.

Hamm counteracts Clov's brazen stunt with a change in his approach. He reintroduces sentimentality and responsibility to increase the level of difficulty that Clov's "ignoring" of the whistle will require: "You won't come and kiss me goodbye?" (45) The affective weight of "kiss me goodbye" is introduced into the dramatic space under the guise of a courtesy: bidding farewell.

Hamm's affectionate words arouse the spectator's curiosity: Is it a sentimental outburst of emotions that were repressed during the rambling course of the representation or a dramatic irony that sends a message to Clov: "Do not let me die in the darkness."?

As the representation inches toward the end, the question of separation intensifies. Clov's increased nervousness and the hobbling of his exit intensify the closure. In a moment of desperation, Clov "*gets down precipitately, looks for the dog, sees it, picks it up, hastens towards Hamm and strikes him violently on the head with the dog.*" (76) In this scene, the toy dog does what Clov failed to do during the course of the play: manifest overtly his wish to cancel Hamm's influence.

The toy dog and Clov share some common features: the dog misses a leg just as Clov is starting to experience problems with his leg, they have both been summoned by Hamm and they kept a low profile during the representation. They also snap out of passivity at the same instant, maul Hamm and inflict a severe blow to his dramatic irony. The toy dog permits Clov to implement physical confrontation into his structural irony.

It is curious that Clov loses his patience when Hamm asks him for the toy dog, while he obeyed humbly a myriad of orders. The search for the perfect center of the room, demanding Clov to bring him a painkiller and questions about the *exact* time or topography did not provoke Clov but the toy dog disrupted his composure.

Hamm metaphorically replaces Clov by asking for the toy dog and his intention triggers the latter's rage. Although Clov wants to disappear into the darkness, a part of him might want to stay by his father's side. It is possible that the toy dog represents a deficient support that can not stand up just as Clov is an unwilling helper that can not stay.

The symbolic severing of the protagonists' strenuous ties with the introduction of the toy dog delivers a blow to Clov's ego. The emotional aspect of the blow adopts the play's reflexive nature, anger is caused by and inflicted upon Hamm. Hamm angers Clov by asking for the toy dog, so Clov transfers his anger back to Hamm by hitting him.

The transference of anger from one protagonist to the other reflects the structure of the play. In other words, the attempt to impose one's view of the situation upon the other in order to establish one's dominance.

Hamm responds to Clov's blow without swaying:

> If you must hit me, hit me with the axe. Or with the gaff, hit me with the gaff. Not with the dog. With the gaff. Or with the axe. (*Clov picks up the dog and gives it to Hamm who takes it in his arms.*) (77)

The toy represents the weapon for the cancellation of Hamm's influence and the symbol of Clov's substitution. And indeed, Hamm embraces the toy dog.

A Possible Cancellation of the Structural Irony

The spectator has observed the power shifts on stage and followed the entangled dramatic threads that might lead to a definite closure of the play. As the dramatic messages roil the spectator's interpretations, the audience gleans tips in order to clarify the drift of *Endgame*. In this search, the stage occupies a loftier place on the ladder of interpretative tips than the protagonists' complex relationships. As the spectator pulls back and looks at the stage from a distance, he discovers a wink that the dramatic space sneaks into the protagonists' performance.

Among the shadows, the spectator observes the protagonists hover between humanity and inanimate matter, one in the wheelchair and the other leaning against the door with a steadfast gaze on his companion. The windows with closed curtains create a sensation of claustrophobia that permeates the stage. The picture, whose face is turned to the wall[19], projects a surrealist view of the scene.

After the spectator has overcome the stupor that the presence of human beings in the trash cans caused, the containers prod anew his curiosity. They become the representatives of the human relations. Nagg and Nell are isolated and at the same time together just like the containers. Beckett ironically places the trash cans one next to the other as if they were shadows of the protagonists and specifies: *"touching each other"*[20]. This contact represents the physical proximity and the mysterious abyss that separates the members of both couples, Nagg and Nell, as well as Hamm and Clov.

The picture that faces the wall offers a glimpse of Clov's state of mind. As an act of restrained rebellion, the picture's position defies the blind master as it refuses to take its customary position: facing the residents. This seditious position is starkly exposed for the audience but it is not visible for Hamm. The hidden picture is a *mise en abîme* of the dramatic space that hides and at the same time shows the forces that regulate the protagonists' complex relations.

---

[19] Beckett. *Endgame*. 1.
[20] Beckett. *Endgame*. 1.

Clov's situation mirrors the picture's position on the wall; they both face the intransigent reality of the wall. Clov desperately longs for new horizons that lie yonder, and the picture can not project its image outward.

Despite the still aspect of the scene, a human manifestation permeates the dramatic space. Brief laughs echo on stage without revealing the person behind it.[21] They comply with the dramatic function of ridiculing Clov's stratagems to severe the *Sisyphus bond* and shackle him to the stage.

From Vellacott's perspective, the laugh could be interpreted as a divide that separates the spectator from the protagonist. It sends a signal to the spectator informing him about the futility of Clov's efforts but Clov remains left out of this communication. The exclusive nature of the laugh's interpretation supports Hamm's dramatic irony.

The initial scene of the play is reproduced in the closure, Hamm is in his wheelchair and Clov is observing him:

> He [Hamm] tries to move the chair, using the gaff as before. Enter Clov, dressed for the road. Panama hat, tweed coat, raincoat over his arm, umbrella, bag. He halts by the door and stands there, impassive and motionless, his eyes fixed on Hamm, till the end. (82)

The resemblance between the initial and final scenes suggests that no change has occurred. In the dramatic space that lies between these two reflecting images, the spectator is the witness of ephemeral guiles that the protagonists displayed.

---

[21] Beckett. *Endgame*. 1.

In the final stage of the play, Hamm cryptically proclaims his victory: "Good". (84); while Clov's focus on Hamm's motionless body confirms the immutable nature of the stage.

He [Hamm] covers his face with handkerchief, lowers his arms to arm-rests, remains motionless. (84)

Hamm has the honor to close the play with a laconic and cryptic statement: "You... remain." (84) His words preserve the dubious nature of the play as the spectator can not conclude with certainty whether "you" refers to Hamm or Clov. Despite this ambiguity, there is a sensation that Hamm succeeded in erecting a wall around himself. Clov continues to hover in the cloud of velleities but opening the door and disappearing in the distance remains in the planning stage. Without really clarifying the protagonists' situation, the spectator becomes the witness of the play's *status quo.*

The rhythm of the protagonists' retorts wanes toward the end of the play. Taking advantage of this breather, the spectator might reconsider the meaning of the play's title by taking into account the ironic context in which the protagonists played their roles. As the title *Endgame* indicates, the representation might be about the final phase of a game. Nevertheless, as the unfolding of the plot is circular and fragmented, the spectator might consider the meaning of the play's title as the "game about the end". Seen from this point of view, the play's meaning changes drastically as the end or Clov's exit is not the final stage of the play but the theme of the game. Beckett has played and continues to play with the spectators proposing alternate interpretations. When the spectator defines a meaning of the play, its opposite emerges. In the syntactic inversion of the key words, "end of the game" and "game about the end", the play responds once more to the ironic paradigm according to which the primary meaning of words indicates the opposite of its hidden message.[22] So, the title of the play and the work that it designates does not have to be understood as the end of the game but as the game about scenes on end.

Bibliography

Beckett, Samuel. *Waiting for Godot*. New York: Grove Press, 1972.

Beckett, Samuel. *Endgame*. New York: Grove Press, 1958.

Booth, Wayne C. *A Rhetoric of Irony*. Chicago: University of Chicago Press, 1974.

Diderot, Denis. *La Paradoja del comediante*. Mexico: Colección Temas Teatrales, 1979.

Frye, Northrop. *Anatomy of Criticism, Four Essays*. New York: Atheneum, 1968.

Glicksberg, Charles Irving. *The ironic vision in modern literature*. The Hugue: Martinus Nijhoff, 1969.

Godin, Georges and La Chance, Michaël. *Beckett, Entre le refus de l'art et le parcours mystique*. Canada: Le Castor Astral, 1994.

Gontarski, Stanley. *The Theatrical Notebooks of Samuel Beckett*. Volume 2: *Endgame*, Grove Press and Faber and Faber, 1993.

Gontarski, Stanley. *The Intent of Undoing in Samuel Beckett's Dramatic Texts*. Indiana UP, 1985.

---

[22] An ironic message contradicts or differs from its literal meaning. See: Hutcheon 173.
Roster 17.
Catherine Kerbrat-Orecchioni. «La ironía como tropo». *De la Ironía a lo grotesco*. Ed. Hernán Silva. Trans. Pilar Hernández Cobos (Mexico: Universidad Metropolitana Iztapalapa, 1992) 196.

Hutcheon, Linda. «Ironía, sátira, parodia. Una aproximación pragmática a la ironía». *De la Ironía a lo grotesco.* Ed. Hernán Silva. Trans. Pilar Hernández Cobos. Mexico: Universidad Metropolitana Iztapalapa, 1992.

Kenner, Hugh. «Shades of Syntax». *Samuel Beckett: a collection of criticism.* Ed. Ruby Cohn. New York: McGraw-Hill Book Company, 1975.

Kenner, Hugh. "Samuel Beckett: Comedian of the Impasse." *The Stoic Comedians, Flaubert, Joyce, and Beckett.* Berkeley, Los Angeles, London: University of California Press, 1974.

Kerbrat-Orecchioni, Catherine. "La ironía como tropo". *De la Ironía a lo grotesco.* Ed. Hernán Silva. Mexico, Trans. Pilar Hernández Cobos. Universidad Metropolitana Iztapalapa, 1992. 195-221.

Kierkegaard, Soren. *The concept of Irony, With Constant Reference to Socrates.* Trans. Lee M. Capel. Bloomington: Indiana University Press, 1968.

Nadeau, Maurice. "Samuel Beckett: Humor and the Void". *Samuel Beckett, A collection of critical essays.* Ed. Martin Esslin. New Jersey: Prentice Hall, 1965. 33-36.

Pavis, Patrice. "Performance analysis: Space, Time, Action". *Gestos, Teoría y práctica del teatro hispánico.* Year 11. N. 22. November 1996.

Roster, Peter J. *La ironía como método de análisis literario: la poesía de Salvador Novo.* Madrid: Gredos, 1978.

Vellacott, Philip. *Ironic drama.* London: Cambridge University Press, 1975.

Worth, Katherine. "The space and the sound in Beckett's theater". *Beckett the shape changer.* Ed. Katherine Worth. London: Routledge & Kegan Paul, 1975. 185-218.

Creation and Cancellation
of Irony in *Happy Days*

Happy Days is one of the most complex and ironic works of Samuel Beckett. It is ironic because it masks the plot and disorients the spectator in his interpretation of the play. Its structure is based on the cancellation of reality and the formation of an illusionary setting[1]. The spectator is faced with the polyvalent structure of the representation in which the stage reality and his anticipation blend together. The dramatic space, austere from the esthetic point of view, absorbs and puzzles the spectator as if the play were based on his personal existential questions.

In the final phase of this essay, we shall see how *Happy Days* creates confusion in the interpretative process with regard to protagonists' intentions and the nature of the dramatic setting.[2] The protagonists' desperation and vain attempts to communicate dissipate in the last scene and the

---

[1] This structure is reflected in:
Soren Kierkegaard. *The concept of Irony, With Constant Reference to Socrates.* Trans. Lee M. Capel (Bloomington: Indiana University Press, 1968)

[2] According to La Chance, the doubt represents an intransigent element in the interpretation of Samuel Beckett's drama.
Georges Godin and Michaël La Chance. *Beckett, Entre le refus de l'art et le parcours mystique* (Canada: Le Castor Astral, 1994)

spectator can sneak a view of Beckett's humanism, which often remains backstage. The play's capacity to show and conceal, as well as to create and annul, reveals the essential principles of irony and its dramatic avatars.

Cancellation of Reality
and the Second Dramatic Level

As the curtain rises, the austere simplicity of the stage unsettles the spectator. An infernal light wreaks havoc on Winnie and blinds the spectator. But the lighting is also revealing as it exposes Winnie's plight. The scorched soil, the pounding sun rays and the protagonist that is buried to the waist open the representation and set the context of the play. The lighting's function is equally significant in the interpretation of the play's title as it sheds ironic light on Winnie's happiness.

The protagonist wakes up and with a ceremonial gesture exposes her face and bosom to the dazzling light. Her words, "Another heavenly day" (8), open the chasm between the protagonist's situation, seen from the spectator's point of view, and her auto-evaluation.[3] Winnie's words contradict the spectator's initial impression and become the leitmotiv of the play. They also remind the spectator that his view is diametrically opposed to those of the protagonist and the literal meaning of the play's title.

The contrasting, interpretative angles meet at the top of the mound where Winnie's buried body lies. The spectator's gaze and the protago-

---

[3] Kenner studies the uncertainty of the protagonist's testimony:
Hugh Kenner. "Shades of Syntax". *Samuel Beckett: a collection of criticism*. Ed. Ruby Cohn (New York: McGraw-Hill Book Company, 1975) 67.

nist's voice vie for the correct interpretation of the play's setting. Is the stage a place of Winnie's suffering or happiness?[4] The point of intersection of the opposite views represents the crux of *Happy Days*.

After the stunning proclamation of happiness, the spectator probes Winnie's obsessive preoccupation with her hairdo. The attention that Winnie dedicates to her hairbrush bestows a fantastic value on this object. The brush moves incessantly from the bag to Winnie's side and back to her bag. The reiterative and meticulously executed gestures give a ceremonious aspect to her activities and intrigue the spectator's analytical perspective.

Winnie does not communicate with the external world because she is surrounded by a mute audience and darkness that lies beyond the stage. In this situation, the mirror offers a valuable feedback about her appearance, well-being and happiness. It also transforms Winnie's soliloquy into an interactive role with herself. At the same time, her reflection is the feedback of the image that she projects to the audience.[5]

The "holy light" (11) and the scorching light that accompany Winnie's sinking into the mound blend in the dramatic space. However, these two concepts remain separate in the spectator's mind as he starts to fol-

---

[4] An obvious contradiction between two points of view could be a sign of an ironic context:

Booth, Wayne C. *A Rhetoric of Irony* (Chicago: University of Chicago Press, 1974) 102.

[5] A considerable number of critics study the dramatic dialogue and its effects:

E. Bentley. *La vida del drama* (México: Paidos Studio, 1982) 77.

Fernando de Toro. «El discurso teatral». *Semiótica del teatro* (Carleton: Editorial Galerna, 1994) 29.

Godin, 43, 48 and 52.

A. Álvarez. *Samuel Beckett* (New York: The Viking Press, 1973) 81.

Ross Chambers. "Beckett's Brinkmanship". *Samuel Beckett, A collection of critical essays*. Ed. Martin Esslin (New Jersey: Prentice Hall, 1965) 167.

low two distinct but parallel paths. The first one is based on the realistic interpretation of the stage setting, while the second deconstructs Winnie's affective side. From this double vantage point, the spectator starts to decipher the representation's ironic context as the protagonist's behavior proves to be incoherent with the dramatic situation.

Winnie's ironic perspective is revealed through her use of the spectacles and the magnifying glass. The alignment of both lenses for the exploration of the mound's fauna brings to mind the structure of a microscope and the intent gaze of a scientist. The study of the ant's appearance and behavior might provoke a spectator's smirk even though the result of the analysis is impressively detailed and verisimilar:

Looks like life of some kind! (*Looks for spectacles, puts them on, bends closer. Pause.*) An emmet! (*Recoils. Shrill.*) Willie, an emmet, a live emmet? (*Seizes magnifying-glass, bends to ground again, inspects through glass.*) [. . .] Ah! (*Follows its progress through grass.*) Has like a little white ball in its arms. [. . .] It's gone in. (*Continues a moment to gaze at spot through glass, then slowly straightens up, lays down glass, takes off spectacles and gazes before her, spectacles in hand. Finally.*) Like a little white ball. (29-30)

The acquisition of information about the ant's location, movement and activity seems absurd despite its accuracy. The fact that the details about the ant occupy Winnie's attention is confounding because she lacks basic information about her husband's dire situation. The irony of the meticulous focus on the ant's burden, "a little white ball", unrolls progressively as if it were tracing the scientist's look that passes through two lenses. The lenses cause a double distortion of dimensions in order to obtain an optical perfection; while on the other hand, Winnie's buried body and her husband's precarious state are eclipsed by the scientific study of the ant.

If the spectator takes into consideration Kierkegaard's cancellation of reality and the creation of a new realm, Winnie's futile activities and declarations acquire highly practical functions.[6] Her comments about happiness, during her sinking into the mound, represent the protagonist's effort to shut her eyes to the conditions of her plight. Behind Winnie's enthusiastic reiteration of the slogan "happy days" and her meticulous observation of the ant with its "little white ball", the spectator discovers Winnie's underlying need to relegate reality to backstage.

The hair dress and the words engraved on the toothbrush contribute to the cancellation of the protagonist's fall into stark reality. Winnie's activities deflect her attention from reality and direct it toward her appearance in the mirror and scenic details like the ant. If she were immersed in a baroque stage setting, in the esthetic and dramatic sense of the word, in which a multitude of protagonists, activities and discourses mingled, the cancellation of reality could have been implemented with a myriad of social modalities and discourses. Nonetheless, in *Happy Days*, the austere setting of the mound requires the active participation of Winnie's imagination to shield herself from reality.

The revolver's presence among beauty articles suggests that it could be confused with brushes and makeup pencils. The revolver could also complement the cancellation of the first dramatic level with the unexpected end of Winnie's life. Its role is similar to the one of the tree in *Waiting for Godot*. They are a constant reminder for the spectator that an alteration of reality could be overshadowed by its total cancellation through the elimination of the protagonists.

Winnie's comments often do not find a receptor and bounce back at her. The reflexive motion of her words forms a soliloquy in which "I" is divided into "concrete I" and "another I". Each side of the "I" reflects

---

[6] Kierkegaard 280.

words toward its counterpart, creating an internal discourse between the two hemispheres of Winnie's mind. The two hemispheres form a hermetic, if not hermeneutic, sphere that leaves out undesirable dramatic elements. The complementarity of the two poles is represented by the mirror whose dynamic reflections, transmitted from and toward the protagonist, correspond to her internal dialogue.

The complementary poles reflect the structure of the play in which the nexus between opposite concepts cements the dramatic unity. They also represent the bond between the concrete and imaginary aspects of the play. The change from the scenic to imaginary concepts is fundamental in Winnie's problematic game as it opens doors for her to the second dramatic level. On the other hand, the spectator has the option of getting involved in the abstract sphere of the play or remaining on the concrete level.

The spectator's possibility to choose one of the two dramatic levels is exclusive as Winnie does not qualify for it. On the concrete or scenic level, the margins of Winnie's possibilities are constrictive and immobilizing. The only option that she has is to cancel the concrete level and enter the second dramatic sphere in which she could continue to avert the cancellation of her role.

> No something must happen, in the world, take place, some change, I cannot, if I am to move again. Willie. (*Mildly.*) Help. (*Pause.*) No? [...] Please, Willie. (*Mildly.*) For pity's sake. (*Pause.*) No? (*Pause.*) You can't.
> [...] Fortunately I am in tongue again. (*Pause.*) That is what I find so wonderful [. . .] (36)

Winnie's soliloquy marks her passage to the second level. On the one hand, it emphasizes the search for a solution in the form of "some change", which is taking an awfully long time to materialize, and it exacerbates the spectator's expectation to see a change on stage. On the other hand, the integral parts of Winnie's "I" manage to establish a metaphysical communication and allow her to *step* momentarily outside the existential bog thanks to a positive view of the world: "That is what I find so wonderful". (36)

Winnie acknowledges the role of words in the creation of the second dramatic level: "Fortunately I am in tongue again." (36) The oral expression or "tongue" allows her to escape from the first level of dramatic existence where the silence threatens her existence as was noted after she beseeched Willie to answer her question. Nevertheless, the "tongue" could also play a confounding role if the game of "singular vs. plural" is applied to it as the spectator witnessed it in Winnie's linguistic elaboration of the word "hair".[7] Adding an "s" to "tongue", the newly formed word could be confused with the tool "tongs". These tongs, like the two sides of Winnie's "I", seize and extract the protagonist from the dreadful silence of the first dramatic level and allow her to float on her phonetic cushion. At the same time, the underlying image of "tongs" suggests a tool that could exert deadly pressure on Winnie that is similar to the one of the mound.

The happy tone of Winnie's voice, "Fortunately I am in tongue again" (36), vibrates with irony as the protagonist finds delight *in tongs*. The mound reflects the ironic tone of her words as it exerts a constant inward pull on Winnie and reminds her of the forces, similar to the tongs, that shape her existence.

During the representation, objects often fill in the gap that the absence of interacting characters has left. They focus, as if they were characters, on Winnie who is the source of and the reason for the cancellation

---

[7] Samuel Beckett. *Happy Days* (New York: Grove Press, 1961) 23.

of the first dramatic level. The objects such as the hairbrush, mirror, hat and makeup contribute to Winnie's dramatic presence and provide her with possibilities. Each object represents a multitude of facets that reflect Winnie's words in the creation of a new world.

Words bounce back at Winnie like objects. Her questions pretend to solicit a response from Willie but the real motivation behind the words is the perpetuation of her soliloquy. The language and the gestures form a duet in whose syncretism echoes the second dramatic level. They serve as the source and continuity of Winnie's mental projection. When she strains her eyes to read the inscriptions that are engraved on her hair-brush handle, her voice is interrupted by pauses that initiate a vehement activity of quick gestures. Thus the pauses cement the links of the *word-gesture-word* chain:

> Fully guaranteed. . . genuine pure. . . (*Pause. Winnie lays down glass and brush, takes handkerchief from bodice, takes off and polishes spectacles, puts on spectacles, looks for glass, takes up and polishes glass, lays down glass, looks for brush, takes up brush and wipes handle, lays down brush, puts handkerchief* [. . .] (17)

When the gestures subside, the words continue.[8] Winnie's alternate impulses, gestures and words digress from the concrete dramatic setting and permit her to build the second dramatic level with the fabric of her imagination, language and objects.

---

[8] Chambers, Álvarez, La Chance and Bentley study the limits and other aspects of the language. They also establish relations between the language and gestures in Beckett's drama.

Chambers 167.

Álvarez 81.

La Chance 89 and 103.

E. Bentley. *La vida del drama* (Mexico: Paidos Studio, 1982) 77.

The source of possibilities that the language offers for the ironic construction of the world, according to Kierkegaard's theory, could be compared with the unfathomable content of the "capacious bag" (7) from which Winnie takes out objects.

The depth [of the bag] in particular, who knows what treasures. What comforts. (32)

The appearance of the revolver that comes out of the bag of niceties represents the emergency exit for Winnie in case the construction of the second dramatic level fails. Unlike other objects, the use of the revolver could bring about the cancellation of both the first and the second dramatic levels. Thus, the presence of the revolver remains an element of absolute cancellation that threatens the continuation of the performance. The extent of its effect is not controllable by the protagonist or the stage, its blast would trigger the fall of the curtain.

At times, silence ensues from the failure of words: "What is one to do then, until they come again?" (24) The pauses reflect Winnie's anguish that she quells with gestures and new linguistic combinations. Both the silence and the revolver remind the spectator that the second level of the dramatic representation might implode and sentence the protagonist to a freefall into permanent silence.

Despite the threat, the revolver and the silence do not cancel the second dramatic level. The revolver remains idle and the silence cedes its place to words. At the self-addressed question about future actions in case words die away, Winnie proposes the use of gestures: "Brush and comb the hair, if it has not been done, or if there is some doubt, trim the nails [. . .]" (24) This suggestion validates the hypothesis about the complementarity between words and gestures in the cancellation of the dramatic reality.

Winnie's relation with objects and words belongs to the gray area between optimism and despair. The ironic optimism about the unfolding of words and gestures maintains Winnie in the game of dramatic creation but her anxiety, like the revolver and silence, affronts head-on her movement toward the second dramatic level. The anxiety's incursion into Winnie's world of fantasy brings into question her survival.

> Shall I myself not melt perhaps in the end, or burn, oh I do not mean necessarily burst into flames, no, just little by little be charred to a black cinder, all this- (*ample gesture of arms*) -visible flesh. (38)

Winnie's realistic contemplation of the situation does not offer any solutions. Her immobility is imposed by forces that she can not sway, while the reason and purpose of her situation remain beyond her and the spectator's mental scope.[9] The lack of information about the hypothetical intention of the superior order that controls Winnie's life does not prevent her from making a practical decision. She implements the principle of cancellation to her prediction about being carbonized. The laconic "no" cancels her anguish or at least represses it in order to adopt her peachy perspective about life that echoes in her exclamation "happy days".

> No. (*Pause*) I speak of temperate times and torrid times, they are *empty words*. (38) [my emphasis]

Winnie's euphoria is often undermined by the elements from the first dramatic level, as dread and death, that she has to take into consideration while constructing her subjective world. She deftly weaves both dramatic

---

[9] The protagonist's incapacity to understand his or her condition:
Charles Irving Glicksberg. *The ironic vision in modern literature* (The Hugue: Martinus Nijhoff, 1969) 44.

levels into the backcloth in which she tentatively shrouds Willie and herself.

> Bless you Willie I do appreciate your goodness I know what an effort it costs you, now you may relax I shall not trouble you again unless I am obliged to, by that I mean unless I come to the end of my own resources which is most unlikely [. . .] (26-7)

Winnie's comments send a stealthy message to the spectator, informing him that the world in which she dwells is the product of her own creation. At the same time she warily contemplates the possibility of her failure in the weaving task: "Unless I come to the end of my own resources".[10] The protagonist discretely informs the spectator about the use of her creative techniques. Winnie's comments are a sign of communication between the opposite sides of the orchestra pit and at the same time an indicator of the protagonist's consciousness about her dramatic transgression from one level to another.

In the previous quotation, Winnie thanks Willie for his effort and the two protagonists unite in their common struggle or at least Winnie creates this similarity to consolidate their unity and continue the fight against dramatic reality.

Willie's exclamation "Fear no more!" (26) manifests his desire to integrate himself in the second dramatic level during Winnie's verbal and affective support. The expression "fear no more" is used by both protagonists and it acquires an ironic dimension in the spectator's interpretation as Winnie and Willie remain far from being safe. Nonetheless, they

---

[10] An interesting comaparison could be established between Winnie's and an actor's imagination by taking into account:

Constantin Stanislavski. *Un actor se prepara* (Mexico: Editorial Diana, 1994) 52.

are at least united in their mental recreation of reality for which even Kierkegaard would congratulate them.[11]

There is an intriguing parallelism between Winnie's and Willie's respective declarations: "mustn't complain, so much to be thankful for" (11) and "Fear no more!" (26) Both statements are structured on cancellation; in the first case, the cancellation focuses on the complaint, and in the second, on fear. By canceling the elements that belong to the first dramatic level, the protagonists create the second level. Their negative statements reflect the scheme of the ironic creation whose first stage is based on the cancellation and the second on creation. By destroying the realm of fear and complaint, they are stepping into the world of subliminal creation. The positive and negative forces are fused in their verbal expressions.

The objects that Winnie uses for the cancellation of reality, such as the mirror, toothbrush and hat acquire a fetishistic dimension as their dramatic value surpasses their function, just as Winnie's wish to have white teeth while she is sinking into the mound seems unreal. Nonetheless, the playing of the common daily roles gives the appearance of a routine lifestyle. These trivial activities incarnate the survival skills that brush aside the life-threatening signs. The toothbrush makes Winnie's teeth shine but their essential role is to create the atmosphere of a "happy day".

The result of the negation and reconstruction of reality is reproduced in Willie's pornographic picture and Winnie's exuberant hat. The objects' esthetic and functional applications pave the road for two felicitous

---

[11] Kerbrat-Orecchioni shows how contradictory aspects of a word and a character blend in irony:

Kerbrat-Orecchioni, Catherine. "La ironía como tropo". *De la Ionía a lo grotesco*. Ed. Hernán Silva. Trans. Pilar Hernández Cobos (Mexico: Universidad Metropolitana Iztapalapa, 1992) 195-221.

trips. In Willie's case, the picture offers a glimpse of carnal pleasures, and in Winnie's, of a luxurious lifestyle. These objects are the integral part of the dramatic setting in which the protagonists play the roles of a happy couple. If the performance proves to be successful from the spectator's point of view, the imaginary and real aspects of the stage will blend and the spectator will enjoy the vacillating view of the second dramatic level.

The fluctuation between the dramatic levels represents the play's ironic structure in which concrete and abstract aspects blend. Winnie's hat and Willie's picture facilitate the dynamic transition from the scenic reality to the second dramatic level. The hat protects Winnie from the sun but its lavish aspect reminds the spectator of the protagonist's fantasy and illusions. Its flowery aspect is complemented by the protagonist's memory, which allows her to establish affective ties with the past experiences. The memory of kisses and dances is reflected in the colorful hat. On the other hand, even though the pornographic picture is firmly anchored in the terrestrial temptations, it offers a shelter within the stage. Thanks to the picture, Willie climbs the dramatic ladder where his mind and body enjoy a refreshing breeze of the second dramatic level.

The protagonists use language, objects and gestures to create an ironic net that they spread out over the dramatic space.[12] When the dramatic elements from the first level invade and endanger the structure of the second level, the protagonists tug on their net in an effort to separate their world from undesirable elements. Winnie's comments about the increasing pressure that the mound exerts on her body are a warning sign

---

[12] About the function of language and objects see:
   Alfred Simon. *Samuel Beckett* (Paris: Pierre Belfond, 1983) 49.
   Alain Robbe-Grillet. «Samuel Beckett, or 'Presence' in the Theater». *Samuel Beckett, A collection of critical essays.* Ed. Martin Esslin (New Jersey: Prentice Hall, 1965) 108.

of the intrusion of reality into the second dramatic level: «The earth is very tight today, can it be I have put on flesh, I trust not.» (28) As an immediate response, a flow of statements allows Winnie to brush aside mentally the irresistible sinking of her body, focus on the ant, and blot out the grim aspect of her situation by playing with the terms "formication" and "fornication". (30) Thus, the words and laughter check the pressure that the reality exerts on the protagonists. While the mound is absorbing Winnie's body, the protagonists are pulling on their ironic net to extract Winnie temporarily from the mound's grip.

The spectator intuitively interprets the protagonists' perspective as incapable of recognizing the intransigent aspect of their situation and their imminent disintegration on the physical and mental levels. At the opening of the second act, the spectator finds an irrefutable proof of the inexorable reality when Winnie's body appears buried to the neck. The lingering image of "happy days" becomes satirical. Facing Winnie and Willie, the spectator deduces that their physical and mental states form a dramatic *collage* of incoherent themes.

Music

Winnie's affective side is reflected toward the orchestra through the music and dance:

> [. . . *Winnie*] *holding box to breast with both hands. It plays the Waltz Duet "I love you so" from The Merry Widow. Gradually* [*Winnie's*] *happy expression.* (39)

While Winnie hugs her musical box and swings her body at the waving rhythm of the melody at the end of the first act, the spectator contemplates the meaning of the waltz. In the context of the protagonist's performance, the happiness and tragedy form a waltzing couple. The line "I love you so" is taken as a description of the widow's mental state that becomes ironic as her husband's demise is inconsistent with her description "Merry Widow". Nonetheless, the incoherence manifests the projection into the second dramatic level. The function of music is similar to the one of objects like the hairbrush because they prop up the protagonists' dramatic structure of escape.

The spectator's interpretation of the dramatic situation is based on Cartesian logic, while the protagonist's contact with the dramatic reality is fantastic. The two perspectives separate the spectator and the protagonist and place them respectively into the realms of reality and illusion.

The spectator anticipates the protagonists' tragic end similar to the widow's destiny. The women share a similar affective situation; just as the widow finds happiness in life despite her husband's death, Winnie encounters joy in another happy day. The spectator seeks the key to the protagonists' enigmatic plight and Winnie seeks an adequate mental flow that would take her on a fantastic journey.

The death of the husband that stems from the waltz is contrary to the ironic creation of the second dramatic level. In case Winnie becomes a widow, the range of options for her verbal creativity would decrease drastically and it would change the conclusion of this chapter. Even though Willie remains hidden and mute during a major part of the representation, he represents the receptor of Winnie's words and gives them a dialectical profile. If he were to die, Winnie would have to erase his demise in order to continue feeling his closeness: "[...] what a joy in any case to know you are there, as usual." (34) Without Willie, the maintaining of the second dramatic level would be more precarious and consequently Winnie's existence would start to spin in circles every time more constricted and centered on the revolver.

The spectator persists in his search for the relation between the waltz and the women's lives. The widow's and Winnie's situations have a similar base; they are happy and their husbands are shrouded in the veil of death. The difference is based on time; the widow already lost her husband and Winnie is on the brink of losing hers. The demise of the husband is vague and through its undefined nature it foreshadows Willie's future. The musical and visual aspects of the two women fuse and the spectator sees them as one. In a similar way, the two husbands become one and he stealthily fades away under the cover of death.

The shrinking number of characters intensifies their dramatic presence through absence. When a smile appears on Winnie's face as she waltzes, it reminds the spectator that the multifaceted image of the protagonist is a byproduct of her own ironic creation. The smile represents a divide between the reality and Winnie's illusory creation. It confounds the spectator and lures him into her domain.

When Winnie appeared buried to the neck at the opening of the second act, the spectator's view of her hopeless situation was confirmed. Nonetheless, his initial distance from the protagonists is absorbed by the dramatic space the way Winnie's body disappeared in the mound. Winnie's unchanged expression of happiness shimmers under the sun as it sets the tone for the second dramatic level:

Someone is looking at me still. Caring for me still. That is what I find so wonderful. (49)

Spectator's Second Dramatic Level

Willie is the only character that shares the dramatic space with Winnie. Nevertheless, in most representations of *Happy Days*, he does not even direct his gaze at Winnie during the first act. The lack of interaction between Winnie and Willie causes an affective emptiness on stage. This vacuous space attracts the spectator's psyche and places it in Willie's shoes. Poor Willie, condemned to anonymity by the stage direction and displaced by the spectator, becomes an observer of the play and drifts metaphorically toward the orchestra. The inversion of the spectator's and Willie's roles is ironic as the spectator does not share Winnie's view about life but is included anyway in her space, while Willie, who is present on stage and in Winnie's affective statements, moves to the orchestra.

The inversion of roles between Willie and the spectator is a part of Winnie's strategy.[13] In the unstable domain of the representation, Winnie manages to create the second dramatic level and usher the spectator into it. She gradually involves the spectator in her game of dramatic creation as he starts to identify himself with the person that Winnie continuously addresses: "Something of this is being heard, I am not merely talking to myself [. . .]" (21) The person who seems to be truly listening to Winnie's soliloquies is the spectator, while Willie drifts away silently. At times, Willie's separation stems from his internal elaboration of the second dramatic level during his contemplation of the pornographic picture; and at others, he is physically outside the spectator's view and irresponsive to Winnie's words.

The spectator lives the dramatic experience on two levels simultaneously. On the one hand, he plays the role of the observer that analyzes

---

[13] Stanislavski describes the relation between the spectator and the character: Stanislavski 166.

Winnie's role. From this perspective, the protagonist's behavior is ironic as it seems inconsistent with her situation. On the other hand, the spectator is incorporated into Winnie's space the way she is being absorbed by the mound. Freed of his body and Cartesian logic, the spectator's psyche comes to rest by Winnie's side.

The spectator's and the protagonist's roles unfold simultaneously on two dramatic levels. In each realm, they develop distinct relationships. On the first level, their views are incompatible; and on the second, a metaphysical complementarity brings them together. If the complementarity did not exist on the second level, the spectator would be excluded from the representation because the dramatic space would be absolutely irrelevant to his affective existence.

The Fall of the Second Dramatic Level

Contrary to the closure of *Waiting for Godot*, an unexpected change occurs in the final scenes of *Happy Days*: the *absent* protagonist, Willie, appears. His tedious clambering to the top of the mound, where Winnie's head still remains above the ground, transforms the internal dynamics of the play. Willie looks steadfastly at Winnie's face and cancels the hypothesis that his attention has been diverted by the pornographic picture, while his tedious crawl toward Winnie brings the representation to its climax.

During his absence from the stage, Willie has honed Winnie's method of cancellation and creation. Now, he grapples with reality in order to mold a new setting.

He drops hat and gloves and starts to crawl up mound towards her. [. .
.] He slithers back to foot of mound and lies with face to ground. (63)

Willie's gaze and clambering incarnate Winnie's notion about the presence of somebody who observes and cares for her. That somebody is no longer a product of her imagination or the spectator's metaphysical projection on the stage. *He* is right there, hugging the mound that is devouring Winnie. Willie does not only reflect Winnie's words but her gestures also; he holds on the mound the way she was hugging a box while swaying to the rhythm of the waltz.

The concept "somebody" represents simultaneously the crystallization of the second dramatic level and its cancellation. "Somebody" surged from Winnie's words but found its identity and place in Willie's role. His appearance expels the protagonist from the stage and the couple is reunited under the radiant light of a happy day. Thus, Willie is the co-founder of the second dramatic level as he creates the idyllic situation that surged from Winnie's byword "happy day". On the other hand, Willie blights the concept of the second dramatic level that was based on Kierkegaard's notion of ironic creation because the setting of a happy day is no longer a product of mental creation but a new reality in the three-dimensional, dramatic space.

From the spectator's point of view, the magical instant or a "happy day" was first a product of Winnie's imagination but Willie's intervention transforms it into the stage setting. Thus Willie completes a circle of transformations; Winnie's projection from reality to the second dramatic level is reversed by Willie's materialization of the "illusion" about a happy day.

With the fall of the second dramatic level, Winnie's words lose their ironic sense. What the spectator saw as Winnie's *illusion*, which Kierkegaard, Hutcheon and other experts in irony describe as one of the fundamental characteristics of irony, becomes the spectator's erroneous interpretation of reality. The illusion becomes a part of the first dramatic level and Winnie's words a prediction of a happy day.

Willie: (*just audible*) Win.

Pause. Winnie's eyes front. Happy expression appears, grows.

Winnie: Win! (*Pause.*) Oh this is a happy day, this will have been another happy day! (64)

Winnie's last words and gaze are focused on Willie, who vindicates his wife's slogan "happy days". Willie's dramatic power, which reaches its peak at the end of the performance, is founded on Winnie's constant references to her husband. By keeping him alive in her statements, Winnie cobbles his path to the final cancellation of the second dramatic level and the couple's dramatic reunification.

Bibliography

Beckett, Samuel. *Waiting for Godot*. New York: Grove Press, 1972.

Beckett, Samuel. *Endgame*. New York: Grove Press, 1958.

Beckett, Samuel. *Happy Days*. New York: Grove Press, 1961.

Álvarez, A. *Samuel Beckett*. New York: The Viking Press, 1973.

Bentley, E. *La vida del drama*. Mexico: Paidos Studio, 1982.

Booth, Wayne C. *A Rhetoric of Irony*. Chicago: University of Chicago Press, 1974.

Chambers, Ross. "Beckett's Brinkmanship". *Samuel Beckett, A collection of critical essays*. Ed. Martin Esslin. New Jersey: Prentice Hall, 1965.

Glicksberg, Charles Irving. *The ironic vision in modern literature*. The Hugue: Martinus Nijhoff, 1969.

Godin, Georges and La Chance, Michaël. *Beckett, Entre le refus de l'art et le parcours mystique*. Canada: Le Castor Astral, 1994.

Kenner, Hugh. «Shades of Syntax». *Samuel Beckett: a collection of criticism*. Ed. Ruby Cohn. New York: McGraw-Hill Book Company, 1975.

Kerbrat-Orecchioni, Catherine. "La ironía como tropo". *De la Ionía a lo grotesco*. Ed. Hernán Silva. Trans. Pilar Hernández Cobos. Mexico: Universidad Metropolitana Iztapalapa, 1992. 195-221.

Kierkegaard, Soren. *The concept of Irony, With Constant Reference to Socrates*. Trans. Lee M. Capel. Bloomington: Indiana University Press, 1968.

Robbe-Grillet, Alain. "Samuel Beckett, or 'Presence' in the Theater". *Samuel Beckett, A collection of critical essays*. Ed. Martin Esslin. New Jersey: Prentice Hall, 1965.

Simon, Alfred. *Samuel Beckett*. Paris: Pierre Belfond, 1983.

Stanislavski, Constantin. *Un actor se prepara*. Mexico: Editorial Diana, 1994.

Toro, Fernando de. "El discurso teatral". *Semiótica del teatro*. Carleton: Editorial Galerna, 1994.

Jacquart, Emmanuel. *Le Théâtre de dérision: Beckett, Ionesco, Adamov*. Paris: Gallimard, 1978.

Kenner, Hugh. "Shades of Syntax". *Samuel Beckett: a collection of criticism*. Ed. Ruby Cohn. New York: McGraw-Hill Book Company, 1975.

Kenner, Hugh. "Samuel Beckett: Comedian of the Impasse." *The Stoic Comedians, Flaubert, Joyce, and Beckett*. Berkeley, Los Angeles, London: University of California Press, 1974.

Kerbrat-Orecchioni, Catherine. "La ironía como tropo". *De la Ironía a lo grotesco*. Ed. Hernán Silva. Trans. Pilar Hernández Cobos. Mexico: Universidad Metropolitana Iztapalapa, 1992. 195-221.

Kierkegaard, Soren. *The concept of Irony, With Constant Reference to Socrates*. Trans. Lee M. Capel. Bloomington: Indiana University Press, 1968.

Muecke, Douglas Colin. *Irony and the ironic*. London: Methuen, 1982.

Nadeau, Maurice. "Samuel Beckett: Humor and the Void". *Samuel Beckett, A collection of critical essays*. Ed. Martin Esslin. New Jersey: Prentice Hall, 1965. 33-36.

Orwell, George. *Animal farm*. London: David Campbell, 1993.

Pavis, Patrice. "Performance analysis: Space, Time, Action". *Gestos, Teoría y práctica del teatro hispánico*. Year 11. N. 22. November 1996.

Peterson, George. "Suffering in modern drama". *Literary Analysis,* Vol. 21. April 1992.

Price, John Vladimir. *The Ironic Hume*. Austin: University of Texas Press, 1965.

Quintiliano, Fabio. *Instituto oratorio*. Trans. Ignacio Rodríguez and Pedro Sandier. Madrid: Hernando, 1942.

Robbe-Grillet, Alain. "Samuel Beckett, or 'Presence' in the Theater". *Samuel Beckett, A collection of critical essays*. Ed. Martin Esslin. New Jersey: Prentice Hall, 1965.

Roster, Peter J. *La ironía como método de análisis literario: la poesía de Salvador Novo*. Madrid: Gredos, 1978.

Rojtman, Betty. *Forme et Signification dans le Théâtre de Beckett*. Paris: Nizet, 1976.

Simon, Alfred. *Samuel Beckett*. Paris: Pierre Belfond, 1983.

Smyer, Richard. *Animal farm: pastoralism and politics.* Boston: Twayne Publishers, 1988.

Stanislavski, Constantin. *Un actor se prepara.* Mexico: Editorial Diana, 1994.

Toro, Fernando de. "El discurso teatral". *Semiótica del teatro.* Carleton: Editorial Galerna, 1994.

Vellacott, Philip. *Ironic drama.* London: Cambridge University Press, 1975.

Villegas, Juan. "De la teatralidad como estrategia multidisciplinaria". *Gestos, Teoría y práctica del teatro hispánico.* Year 11. N. 21. April 1996.

Wellershoff, Dieter. "Failure of an Attempt at De-Mythologization: Samuel Beckett's Novels". *Samuel Beckett, A collection of critical essays.* Ed. Martin Esslin. New Jersey: Prentice Hall, 1965.

Worcester, David. *The Art of Satire.* New York: Norton, 1969.

Worth, Katherine. "The space and the sound in Beckett's theater". *Beckett the shape changer.* Ed. Katherine Worth. London: Routledge & Kegan Paul, 1975. 185-218.

Wright, Edward. *Para comprender el teatro actual.* Mexico: Fondo de Cultura Económica, 1978.